SHAKESPEAREAN MOTIVES

Shakespearean Motives

Derek Cohen
Associate Professor of English
York University, Ontario

St. Martin's Press   New York

First published in the United States of America in 1988

Printed in Hong Kong

ISBN 0–312–01267–5

Library of Congress Cataloging-in-Publication Data
Cohen, Derek.
Shakespearean motives / Derek Cohen.
p. cm.
Bibliography: p.
Includes index.
ISBN 0–312–01267–5 : $29.95
1. Shakespeare, William, 1564–1616–Characters. 2. Characters
and characteristics in literature. I. Title.
PR2989.C6 1988
822.3'3—dc19   87–12532
                                                          CIP

To Marjorie

Contents

Acknowledgements   8

1   Introduction   9
2   The Rites of Violence in *1 Henry IV*   22
3   *Measure for Measure* and the Drama of Pornography   36
4   The Transforming Audiences of *Richard II*   53
5   The Alternating Narratives of *Twelfth Night*   72
6   Modes of Story Telling in *Othello*   88
7   Shylock and the Idea of the Jew   104
8   The History of *King Lear*   119

Notes   134
Index   141

Acknowledgements

The chapter on *The Merchant of Venice* appeared in a slightly different form in the *Shakespeare Quarterly* (Spring 1980) and then on *1 Henry IV* in the *Shakespeare Survey* (1985). I should like here to record an old debt to Professor J. Max Patrick, formerly of New York University. For their support I thank Sam, Sophie, Anita and Barney Cohen and Marjorie Cohen to whom this book is dedicated.

1 Introduction

The variety of approaches to the plays studied in this book will not, I hope, obscure my central interest in characterization. I do not wish to propose definitive criticisms of the plays or the characters I discuss; rather, I offer 'readings' of the characters from different perspectives. In reading, reading about, and teaching Shakespearean drama, I have found myself constantly drawn back to the question of how what happens in the plays – in the many senses of the phrase – is interesting to me chiefly in what it tells about Shakespeare's characters. Thus, despite my discrete emphases in the following chapters upon such apparently incongruous subjects as Shakespeare's use of language, ritual, narrative, psychological and social motivation, I have kept before me at all times the idea that these matters, however vitally evident, are also ways of seeing character. They function, in a sense, as the means through which dramatic character may be critically observed and, in each case, propose a different angle of observation of the same general subject.

It is probably true to say that there are as many different characters inside any of Shakespeare's major and minor characters as there are actors to play them and readers to read their parts. One might take this assertion a logical step further. If each character is seen differently by each reader, it must follow that each character is seen differently by each reader upon each reading. This is surely so because while the character in the drama is forever fixed, the reader of that character is forever changing, and thus his reading of that character's part is inevitably altered by his application of his altered self to the text. This can be easily seen in the more obvious exercise of criticism. A text can upon a reading – first, second, or fifth – seem to yield a meaning and the critic can convey his understanding of that meaning by writing it out in the form of a critical essay. However, the reading of another criticism about the same text can greatly change the once certain understanding just as it can simply confirm belief in the same earlier reading. Less obviously, but no less surely, the critic himself upon his re-reading of the text is an older and slightly or considerably altered critic. The difference in him between the two readings may not be reflected in his articulation of the reading – in his writing or thinking about the text – but it is undeniable.

The dramatic character, on the other hand, as in one sense a merely mechanically functioning unit in a larger scheme, is ultimately a fixed entity. He is limited in the way that no human being is limited, is typical or, even, symbolic, in the way that no human begin can be and is absolutely whole and knowable in the way that no human being is either. The 'knowableness' of the character in a play, while theoretically possible, is nevertheless practically subservient to the infinite variety of those who would know him. That is, while the fixedness of the dramatic character is indisputable, he cannot ultimately be wholly known simply because the lives and experiences of him of those who read, hear or see him are essentially different. He is perceived differently by each 'reading' of him. When, as often happens, certain readings of certain characters or plays take hold, all that is reflected in the fact of the dominance of an interpretation is a willingness of readers to be persuaded by another reader. This willingness can, obviously, stem from a variety of causes such as social climate, social opinion, political and economic necessities, psychological compulsion, to name but a few. The case of Shylock is instructive in this regard. Ages passed when it was normal to read Shylock as the embodiment of villainy and to recognize his Jewishness as merely one more component of it. The nineteenth century, with its romantic and, to some extent sentimental, predilections, discovered another Shylock, the one Shakespeare *really* meant – a persecuted member of an oppressed race. This Shylock was embraced by the age and became the dominant Shylock of the period. Today, in a world which venerates Shakespeare unquestioningly, and which has seen the nearly successful attempt to exterminate the Jewish race in its recent past, that reading of Shakespeare's Jew remains dominant for the reason that anti-Semitism has become unacceptable ideology while in the eyes of readers, audiences and critics Shakespeare continues to be regarded as incapable of moral error. The Shakespeare of today, in keeping with the dominant political value of Western society, is racially tolerant, a feminist, against war. That is, we, his readers, have made him over in our image. Shakespeare's plays have been too subtle for us. It is salutary to recall that these same plays have been pressed into the service of fascist regimes throughout the world as reflecting *their* values. Our typical reprehension of this 'abuse' of the poet is, we need to recall, merely a theoretical position itself. We are arguing that we are right and 'they' are wrong about 'our' poet.

The strong feelings aroused by the question of what Shakespeare means derive from the problem of how he means his characters, and it is in the different 'knowings' of the characters that different interpretations as to the meaning of Shakespeare arise. A dramatic character has no secret, no undisclosed past and no hidden depth though he may assert their presence. Every word he speaks, has ever spoken, will ever speak is heard, overheard and read, every thought recorded. He is, in a concrete sense, a composite of *données*, of words spoken by and about him, of gestures indicated by these words, of relations to others similarly composed. And yet, despite this palpable known existence, we continue to insist by our reading of the dramatic character that he is essentially a mystery, and that the palpability of the character is merely the touchstone of his inner life. Thus, though a character does or says this or that in real measureable terms, the mystery resides in how we understand what he means by what he does or says because we are different from each other. The whole of the character is an aggregate of signs – of single words, speeches, expostulations, ejaculations, movements – and open to a range of understandings that is probably infinite. Certainly one of the practises of criticism is to make sense of some of the variations and combinations of elements which are possible within the scope of the drama in which the character is engaged. Though the multiplicity of variations and combinations is theoretically finite, in practise the possible combinations of relations of elements of the character and the play – say, word to word, idea to idea, gesture to gesture, word to gesture, idea to word *et cetera* – within the play and to the reader, critic, actor and director is unending. Thus, to pluck the heart of the character is problematic not merely because there is no solution to his mystery but because there is no resolution of the fact that those who would subject the character to the laws of comprehension are themselves quintessentially compounded of different matter.

The problem is demonstrable by reference to the acknowledged difference between flat and round characters. What distinguishes the two types of characters in a narrative is truly a function not merely of their likeness to life or their fullness of personality. Rather the distinction lies quite simply in the way in which we, the readers and observers of these characters, respond to them – in their sheer and purely subjective interestingness to us: that is to say, in a consensus about the fascination which they hold for us. We may note that as criticsm as a profession has burgeoned it has slowly but surely begun to accord those characters in literature who were once dismissed or ignored more and more significance so that they, these marginal characters, are slowly moving into the focus of critical attention and being accorded the kind of deference once reserved for those characters whom consensus declared to be indisputably major or round. What determines a character's flatness is not necessarily anything inherent in the character so nominated, but rather the reader's or the spectator's or the director's decision that the character is flat. After all, surely the only way in which the flat character differs from the round character – as these old-fashioned terms imply – is that there is less of him. But the common agreement of his readers about his function is the final arbiter of his insignificance, and this common agreement is reached only upon the purely subjective decision that he is not interesting to those who read his part.[1] His readers agree that there is no scope for interpretation of the part of the flat character, and they agree upon his function.

In Act IV, scene vii, line 36 of *Hamlet*, a messenger enters with letters and announces, 'These to your Majesty, this to the Queen.' To Claudius's response, 'From Hamlet! Who brought them?' the messenger replies, 'Sailors, my lord, they say. I saw them not./They were given me by Claudio. He received them/Of him that brought them.'[2] Having handed over the letters the messenger is ordered out of the king's presence never to return. This messenger, a character in *Hamlet*, has delivered in his two lines the whole of himself and, so far as I know, has not ever been the subject of critical interest as even a minor character in Shakespeare. This neglect of him seems to add up to a consensus that his character never escapes from the purely functional and steroetypical limits which his role places upon him. As one of drama's functionaries, he is related by his readers to the type from which he derives – one of life's functionaries: a man of no power or importance in his occupation, he is patronized, ordered about, unnoticed by his superiors, used, abused and neglected. He is allowed no emotional life, no family, no home, no friends. The words he speaks and those spoken to him are the entirety of his life. There is simple agreement about his function and character among all who read his lines or see his part. And there is probably no reader or spectator in any culture whose philosophical, ethical, or political assumptions are such as to make him perceive the messenger in a different way from that in which he has always been perceived by readers and critics. Even if the messenger is understood to be a lackey of the feudal/capitalist system of the Danish court, his character has never been altered by the assumption. But this is only because he has failed to *interest* those who read him in himself. Indeed, given the highly charged context of the drama into which he is momentarily introduced it is part of his function not to draw attention to himself. And yet, it seems to me premature to assume that the critical neglect to which such 'functional' characters have been subjected up to now is to be their fate for all time. May we not, for example, reasonably make some heavyish weather of the fact that the unseen messenger who provided our messenger with the letters which he received from the sailors who brought them possessed nearly the same name as the king he is presently addressing? Suddenly, and for no obvious reason Shakespeare brings to the forefront of the dialogue a curiously indirect allusion to the *name* of the villain of the play who is physically present. And this allusion – with its dramatic and linguistic consequences – is accomplished by the use of a dramatic character who has no physical existence in the drama.

The protagonist in the play, however, is continuously interesting in precisely the way that the messenger is uninteresting. Because we are provided with a rigidly determined, fixed, unalterable life story, consisting of a complex and varied set of relationships to others, to ideas, roles and functions, we are also provided with the implication of an alternative to each of the aspects of the story. The drama, that is, becomes dynamic in relation only to the fact of the reader or spectator. The event which is fixed by the protagonist's story as it is worked out in the course of the drama calls attention to itself, in part, because its actual occurrence implies an alternative occurrence. So the play is interesting on one level because it suggests the hypothetical existence of another, or several other possible occurrences. And the character is interesting to us individually in proportion to his capacity to evince from us the image of things happening otherwise. Unlike Claudius's messenger, the protagonist, whose life is drawn with large and vivid strokes, absorbs us because we tend egotistically to see aspects of our own lives in his. The story of the life of the dramatic character is the story of that character's identity, as our own lives are the stories of how we wittingly and accidentally determine those structures by which we define our own identities. As the dramatic character's story is an account of his relationships with others and a consequent and continuous recognition of how his self is reordered and restructured by these relationships, so our own lives are stories of the consequences of the reconciliations and compromises necessitated by social relationships. Our identities are determined by our physical circumstances and the ways in which we adjust to them. We recognize in others around us, as dramatic characters are made to recognize in those around them, that others have identities too. The tendency to categorize those others is a way of simplifying the eternally perplexing matter of the form of that entity we call self. Thus calling Shylock 'the Jew', as almost every character in the play does, is a means of simplifying both his and their existences in the terms by which he relates to the speaker's self. The act of so naming him by reference to what he is rather than by reference to who he is deprives him of the complexity of the humanity by which the speakers define themselves.

But this is only an egregious example of the human tendency, demonstrated in the plays, to comprehend the self through the means of others. When Lear banishes Cordelia, the fury he exhibits derives not merely from the fact that his proleptic fantasy of a quiet retirement has been thwarted, but because the assumptions of his relationship with Cordelia have been redefined. He is made to see that the world around him is not the semi-static social order of his solipsistic imagination, but that it consists, in a way he has not heretofore recognized, of living, breathing human beings who insist, like him, upon the right to fathom their own identities and who refuse, like him, to accept simplifying definitions of themselves. Thus, when Lear faces the crisis of disappointment which Cordelia's refusal provokes, he is seeing her as several simplified personae which together do not explain the events of the present. Cordelia is, and always has been in his eyes, a series of stereotypes: she is daughter, she is favourite daughter, she is subservient daughter, she is marriageable daughter, nursemaid, mother. Notably, she is not a dynamic separate individual but a composite of types which confirm Lear's idea of himself. When Cordelia refuses to cooperate, Lear simply reverses the flat coin to discover its other side, another stereotype, the ungrateful daughter. His rage stems from the violation done to his self, from the discovery that the simplified external world and its relations are mutable and unfixed. Lear's world is a New Critic's text – an ultimately knowable entity –

if only he can find the right code. But the play insistently brings him to the brink of the more hurtful discovery that the text whose secret he keeps trying to grasp is irreducibly complex and ultimately insubordinate to the critical rules he summons. Cordelia, unlike her sisters, cannot accept her father's demand because, unlike her sisters, she recognizes and, in her refusal to speak as he wishes her to, acknowledges Lear's full and multivalent humanity. To Regan and Goneril, Lear is the old king whose feelings must be assuaged by flattery; in this impression they differ very little from the other Britons surrounding the monarch, or, for that matter, from the monarch himself. To Cordelia he is both king and father. For her to follow the example of her sisters is to engage in the deception by which his simplified conception of the world is supported.

To Cordelia, Lear is a fully complex human being. She treats him as a father, as a man whom she has always known. She treats him as though she knows things about him which they share from old. To Cordelia, according to the conventions of Shakespearean realism upon which her character is partly based, Lear is as real as any real father. In other words, while Lear is in fact a fixed and definitive entity, to his daughter he is as complex as a father. She shows knowledge of a Lear we can never know, and yet, as her surprise suggests, she does not fully know him. She relates to Lear on the basis, not only of what occurs between them when they are together, but on that of lives shared elsewhere and at other times where they have no existence for us. Thus the difficulty of comprehending dramatic characters like these – rounded and multidimensional – is the paradoxical difficulty of probing a nonexistent world of experience upon which the understandings of the characters are based. When Cordelia tells her father, 'You begot me, bred me, lov'd me,' (I,i,96) she is making that past real life real and relevant. But there is little else of the past for the reader than such shadowy and generalized allusion. For the shaping experiences of the relationship here between father and daughter are apprehensible through the spontaneous expression of present feeling. Through such passionate phrases as 'Hence and avoid my sight!' (I,i,123) or 'Now, our joy' (I,i,82) does Lear vivify that unknowable past time by the most ephemeral and ineffable of allusions. The feeling, that is, surmounts the simplification to which he is so compulsively subject. Just as in *Hamlet*, the absence of apparent passion in Claudius's messenger measurably and proportionately reduces his stature and makes more discernible the fixedness and limitations on his dramatic personality.

An additional dimension of character becomes evident when the character self-consciously devotes himself to justifying and explaining who he is and what he has become by direct reference to the unknowable past, to that unseen part of his life which has been lived through and has moulded the present and evident self. Othello, for example, is constantly attempting both to explain and understand the self he has become by virtue of the life he has already lived before the beginning of the play. Indeed, his history may be an example to us of how little it is possible fully to know one's own past. Certainly, in his almost compulsive allusion to the life he has known, the adventures he has had, the tribulations he has suffered, Othello shows himself to have reordered the events of his life into neatly complete and perhaps too straightforward and uncomplex narratives. A consequence for him is the impossible balancing of a simple and tidy understanding – even a nostalgic one – of the old days with a perplexing present that refuses to be accommodated to the Procrustean bed he attempts to fit it to.

On the other hand, the play is a narrative, and therefore is, by definition, obedient to the temporal laws of that form. It has its own past, present, and future moments, and it is within these that its characters, in all their completeness, find form over time. Fixed though they may be, they nevertheless have a lasting existence in which change becomes possible. The cause of the development of character is in essence the fact of the passage of time itself. As events alter over time, so the character in a play must confront the dynamic situation as its changing conditions relocate him in the world he inhabits. That relocation can be gentle, almost imperceptible, or it can be radical. In the latter case, that faced by most of the protagonists in Shakespeare's dramas, the stable structures of the past, of living normally and diurnally, are fractured or completely destroyed and new orientations and visions become needful to the continuance of life. Indeed, even in the tragedies where death awaits, that great fact is always preceded by the protagonist's recognition that until death, however near he knows it to be, the future has got to be faced on new terms, in new ways and upon bases that must be newly formed in the light of the destruction of the old. Richard II, uncrowned, has to live in a world of which he is not king. The foundation of faith, of function, even of social relationships has been removed. The very means of his self-apprehensions have been destroyed. And thus, for him, a crucial discovery dependent upon the passage of time through the process of suffering is the recognition that his own past self is integrally linked to the self which he now faces in the presence of the newly powerful Bolingbroke. That is, though he has been overthrown by forces outside of himself, though his physical and material fortunes have been reversed, he cannot truly separate that early self from the events which have culminated in the present crisis. The crisis, whose central moment is Richard's discovery of an inner being bound to the exterior monarchical persona by which his world was defined, links the whole man to the whole world of which he discovers himself to be a part. The discovery is the essence of the character Richard becomes before his death. Necessary to the tragic enlightenment which this play provides, it is dependent upon a narrative structure which shows the passages through destruction and reconstruction of the bases of the self as it faces change.

Adaptation to present circumstances is, of course, immanent to drama as it is to life. Even the resistance to change, the apparent refusal to adapt in acknowledgement of change is a tacit, if reluctant, adaptation. In *Twelfth Night*, for example, Malvolio emerging from his prison discovers that the whole world has realigned itself in his absence; he can do little other than spit out a threat of revenge in response. The threat implies a challenge to the very elemental force of life, time itself. The threat proposes a reversal of time, a return to an order from which he is not excluded, a return, if possible to enjoyment of power. There is sad comedy in the sheer futility of the menacing steward departing from the stage. Similarly, but somewhat more gravely, the last glimpse we are given of Shylock shows a profoundly sudden reversal of the whole of his tendency towards power and threat. In their last moments, he and Malvolio are in the irreconcilable positions of simultaneously being the villains and the victims of their plays.

The fact is that all characters in all plays have to adapt to the changes brought about by the playwright. Part of the interest of Shakespeare's major characters is that of observing the ways in which the drastic or the slowly evolving alteration of conditions affect them. Viola's story in *Twelfth Night* involves the reader in a singularly intriguing way. By assuming her disguise she attempts to entrap and contain time, for the disguise posits the implication that once it is removed she will revert to the character she was before she put it on. But it is surely the sheer impossibility of reverting to old understandings and old conditions that strikes ever more deeply at her heart during the course of the play. The disguise does nothing to freeze time; instead it places her at further and further removes from the self she knew before she adopted it. We are witness to the private life and growth of Viola's self. As Cesario – who must be destroyed before the end of the play – she reveals herself unable to stop the rush of time and of the potentially destructive event of the agonizing growth of her love for Orsino. As the play continues, as time passes, Viola shows with her every breath that her feelings for Orsino grow deeper and that, as a result, she can never return to being the innocent young virgin who survived the shipwreck in the first act.

Viola is caught in a trap of her own devising on the one hand and of the devising of nature on the other. She is a woman, and the disguise is a certain attempt to overcome the limitations which the fact of gender places upon her in Illyria. But in the story of her life nature conquers all, and the magic of comedy, by which any transformations of spirit and body are possible to effect its happy endings, brings a traditional harmony of sexual type and function to effect the play's resolution. Notwithstanding the ambiguity of its sexual ideology, the play's resolution is dependent upon simplified notions of femininity which are incarnated in Viola's nurturing and life-giving sweetness of spirit to which all thoughts are bent through the drama and by which all other sexual types are judged and found wanting in the end.

Not so, however, Isabella in *Measure for Measure*, where the prevailing notions of sexuality and gender are subjected to astringent testing and where the consolations of such stereotypes as exist in *Twelfth Night* are overturned and re-examined. Where *Twelfth Night*'s ideas of sexuality are the typical comic ideas of sex as the basis of happy, crude, exciting, and titillating drama, in *Measure for Measure* Shakespeare takes the matter of sex and its power over behaviour to the extremes to which he takes it in *King Lear*. Angelo is a kind of sane mad King Lear. Sex is human nature's weapon of self-destruction; in this play it is subversive wherever it exists. Even the blameless Claudio calls it a 'thirsty evil'. (I,i,122). At the source of all action in the play, sex is thing that is manifest. It is the immediately relevant fact in the lives of the participants in this social tragedy, and it is to the question of sexuality that attention is turned. Though Vienna is a society disoriented by sexual license, Duke Vincentio places the responsibility of recovering social order in the hands of a sexual misfit. The calamitous consequences of this

olitical decision, whose ramifications extend beyond the official
nding of the play – Angelo and Isabella have memories – derive
om the inevitable and natural fusions of the social and the sexual
1 gender-determined matters of power and its lack. That Angelo
hould associate feelings of sexuality with the exercise of tyranny is
fact that is bound as much to his maleness as to the fact that he is
1e Duke's surrogate. That his confusion of these social and sexual
lements of himself should take form in pornographic desires to
ubjugate is a logical outcome of the stresses which Shakespeare
as located at the heart of this play. The main stress takes shape
om the collision of the two main characters involved in the
ncounter between the male and female worlds and the assump-
ons each brings to bear on the conflict. That is, while the play is
bout sex in the sense of the sexual act and its implications for
1dividual behaviour, it is equally about the contending notions of
ender in the sense of sexual roles having socially crucial impli-
ations about power and equality. The sex/gender conflict domi-
ates many of the dramas and performs a major part in determin-
tions of character. Angelo's life as a dramatic character is directly
ependent upon the existence of Isabella who completes him. In the
ame way we think of many of the great characters of Shakes-
earean drama as gender-dependent parts: Viola and Orsino, and
)thello and Desdemona, for example, are individually separable
haracters but simultaneously they are dependent upon each other
or full dramatic life, both from the point of view of the narrative
vhich binds their histories and from the way in which each of them
s psychologically affected by the fact of the existence of the other.
1 cases like these it is necessary to consider the effect of sex, as it
nks the characters, and gender as it separates them; each
ndividual, engaged in the life of the other, is solipsistically
mpelled to assumptions about the other because of his or her own
ender and because of assumptions about the gender of the other.

   In the sense that the conflict between individuals possesses a
ocial dimension incorporating society's prejudices and ideals,
ender-determined behaviour is related to the abstract and meta-
hysical element of character. The character embodies and
epresents a complex of the ideologies of the world he or she
nhabits, and it is in the attempt to unravel the tightly woven
hreads of self that the character more and more nearly encounters
he sheer difficulty of individual identity. Individuality is hedged
vith unconscious and conscious awareness and understanding of

the world: in striving to come to terms with the world, the characte
attempts to make sense out of the fusion of ideologies and impulse:
which constitute the self. He can be seen, as in *Hamlet*, struggling t
comprehend his own soul by reaching deeply into the darke
recesses of the self and drawing into the light of understanding th
most secret and mysterious elements of his humanity. Or he can be
seen with less awareness and less pain, like Prince Hal locked in
contention with his own father, trying to sort out and simplify hi
locus in the relationship by reference to the customs and ideologica
forms which bind individuals to each other. Prince Hal's problem –
and he recognizes it as such – is to replace the habitual and earned
distrust of his father for himself with faith and love. To accomplisl
this, to purchase trust and love, he invokes the timeless rituals o
violence and sacrifice as evidence of his worthiness. His story thu:
centres upon the social ideology of cleansing the self of the stain:
which time has put upon it. His character is revealed through the
determination to pursue, and the final accomplishment of, the
ritual of cleansing through the exhibition of worthiness in a life
risking enterprise. Prince Hal's quest demonstrates the sheer out
sideness of his character. He is difficult to grasp because we see him
from the outside almost all of the time. He is a nimble-footed
adapter to circumstances and capable of rising to all of the occasion:
with which his life is informed. But in the two scenes in *1 Henry IV*
in which he is seen privately, his talk takes the form not of intro
spection but of address; that is, he is conscious of speaking to ar
audience. On the first occasion that audience is quite explicitly the
theatre audience; on the second it is the dead Hotspur and the
apparently dead Falstaff. In neither case does Hal overtly investi-
gate (though he does reveal) his own motives or his inner self. The
social forms are his chief concern: we may thus assume that in the
play, certainly, they are Shakespeare's dominant interest, even ir
the difficult and individualistic matter of character delineation. The
transactions with the self displayed by the chief character in *1 Henry
IV* are of a kind that advert to the social rather than the individua
values – they tend to place the individual speaker into a direc
relationship with his fellow men and thus locate him ethically
within a social context. The constant reference to the outside world
in this play argues a concern with the individual's social characte
which is somewhat different from the tragedies and *Measure fo
Measure*, for example, where Angelo's assumption of the equani-
mous relationship between the outer and inner selves is severely

ried and challenged by the events of his life and where the
mphasis is placed upon the separation of these aspects of his
dentity.

A play is perhaps as complex a phenomenon as its author a
˻uman being. Being essentially mysterious, it is subject to as varied
eading, strategies of comprehension, and methods of analysis as a
˻uman. And ultimately it is as resistant to complete or definitive
nowing. That is, the theory by which analysis can yield complete
nd certain knowledge of its subject is merely an ideological effort
o place and keep human production under human control in ways
hat the human being – his body and mind – can never be. Once the
vork acquires apparently objective form, that of words on paper,
nd the resultant capacity to be bought and sold, borrowed and
tolen, it gives the illusion of being potentially submissive to
ontrol. The readings of character in the following chapters are, like
nuch criticism, a paradoxical attempt to comprehend their
nysteries in full awareness of the ultimate irreducibility of the
·lements of art. Their limitation is an acknowledged concern with
he questions of identity as they relate the characters of the plays
liscussed to the worlds which they inhabit. Each play has its own
vorld, each world its own structures, each structure its own rami-
ications and, hence, each character as he is defined or as he defines
˻imself in his world does so uniquely. The conventions he acknow-
˻edges and the language he uses bind him to his world – to his
riends and enemies in it – as utterly as they separate him from
ither worlds and other structures. In discussing the plays individually, I have attempted to identify that aspect of the play and its
vorld which seems to me a peculiarly appropriate means through
vhich to examine the question of character in the individual
lrama: that aspect which has suggested itself to me as an apposite
vay of seeing the play as it illuminates the characters I have chosen
o examine.

2 The Rites of Violence in *1 Henry IV*

Hotspur is a character whose career runs the gamut of dramatic expression. Commencing on a note of furious, even farcical, comedy, his life concludes on a note of tragic grief so poignantly realized as to have inspired Northrop Frye's perception that his dying remark 'thoughts, the slaves of life', comes out of the heart of the tragic vision.[1] Hotspur's brave death is placed squarely and deliberately before the audience and provides the final means by which they can comprehend the nature and meaning of his life. Gradually the character has been moulded and determined by forces and events that culminate in the great encounter between himself and Prince Hal. The forces, both those seen by and those hidden from Hotspur, are the means by which the audience and reader are able to apprehend and absorb the development of a character whose existence has been bent into the shape of tragic suffering shown by that last speech:

> O Harry, thou hast robb'd me of my youth!
> I better brook the loss of brittle life
> Than those proud titles thou hast won of me;
> They wound my thoughts worse than thy sword my flesh:
> But thoughts, the slaves of life, and life, time's fool,
> And time, that takes survey of all the world,
> Must have a stop. O, I could prophesy,
> But that the earthy and cold hand of death
> Lies on my tongue: no, Percy, thou art dust,
> And food for –
>
> (V, iv, 76–85)

This speech, to which I shall return, is the apotheosis of Hotspur. By virtue of the transmogrifications wrought in drama through deliberately vivid depictions of dying moments, Hotspur becomes, during this quiet, nearly still, moment in the play, hero, god, and sacrificial creature of society.[2] The fallen hero speaking and looking

22

upwards at his conquerer commands the world he has lost just as he leaves it; and he does so in a manner and with a completeness that have been denied him up to now. It is the concentration of the audience's, the reader's, the prince's passive energy upon the spectacle of the dying soldier that emphasizes his role as the sacrificial victim of his and our world – a transcendence which involves us with his conqueror and his society in a silent collusion in the sacrifice. The production and reproduction of this play over the centuries testifies to a persisting pleasure (aesthetic and moral) in what is arguably the central emotional event of the drama.

Hotspur's death, a palpable and carefully prepared ritual, is directly referable to Prince Hal's vow of fealty to the king, his father.

> Do not think so; you shall not find it so:
> And God forgive them, that so much have sway'd
> Your Majesty's good thoughts away from me!
> I will redeem all this on Percy's head,
> And in the closing of some glorious day
> Be bold to tell you that I am your son;
> When I will wear a garment all of blood,
> And stain my favours in a bloody mask,
> Which, wash'd away, shall scour my shame with it:
> And that shall be the day, whene'er it lights,
> That this same child of honour and renown,
> The gallant Hotspur, this all-praised knight,
> And your unthought-of Harry chance to meet.
> For every honour sitting on his helm,
> Would they were multitudes, and on my head
> My shames redoubled! For the time will come
> That I shall make this Northern youth exchange
> His glorious deeds for my indignities.
> Percy is but my factor, good my lord,
> To engross up glorious deeds on my behalf;
> And I will call him to so strict account
> That he shall render every glory up,
> Yea, even the slightest worship of his time,
> Or I will tear the reckoning from his heart.
> This, in the name of God, I promise here:
> The which, if he be pleas'd I shall perform,
> I do beseech your Majesty may salve
> The long-grown wounds of my intemperance:

If not, the end of life cancels all bands,
And I will die a hundred thousand deaths
Ere break the smallest parcel of this vow.

(III, ii, 124–59)

The power of the speech derives not only from the solemnity of the vow and its invocation of the imagery of blood sacrifice, but also from the variegation of mood within it. The telling first line contains a note of beseeching which hovers on the verge of the imperative. It takes strength from its repeated negatives and urgent exhortation: 'Do not think so; you shall not find it so': – the first 'so' neatly dividing the line and balancing with the second in a parison of rhythm and harmony of logic. The monosyllables of the line, coming as they do immediately after King Henry's latinate, almost otiose, 'degenerate', emphasize the contrast between the speakers.

Hal's speech is the climax of the play in the sense that here the death of Hotspur is given substance and form as an inevitable consequence of what is occurring between the king and the prince.[3] Thus is the destruction of Hotspur by Hal transformed from a shadowy probability into a central fact of the play. It is the fact by which Hotspur becomes the ritual object of a revenger's quest. Resolution through death, as Lawrence Danson argues, 'is necessary to assure the sort of enduring memorial [the hero] and his creator seek, and is an integral part of the play's expressive form'.[4] This shift in emphasis from the probable to the actual takes force less from the known historical details on which the play is based than from the nature of the sacred vow, taken in private and hedged with such images of bloodshed as are traditionally identified with ancient, pre-Christian rites of purification.

As the willing captive of drama's most private moments and thus the willing possessor of the secret thoughts and desires of characters in a play, the audience becomes, perforce, a collaborator in the action. That is, the mere fact of silent observation of a ceremony (social, religious, theatrical) compels one into a posture of collusion. That the audience is forced to collude in Hal's oathtaking is a consequence of the natural, but nonetheless dramatically contrived, fact of Hotspur's absence which further separates the warrior from the ethical circle of 'right' action to which the audience is willy-nilly a party. The confrontation of father and son, with its ramifying features of paternal accusation leading directly to the solemn blood oath, is a reenactment of a mythical encounter, a direct step towards purification in a blood ritual through which society itself will be saved. The blood images of this speech are unlike almost all of the other blood images in the play. Where those elsewhere are emotionally and morally neutral, in Hal's vow the images of the bloody mask and the garment all of blood harness the full force of traditional, even archetypal, mythic sanctity. Hal's promise to redeem himself by shedding Percy's blood is the moment to which the play has logically tended from his first soliloquy – 'I know you all . . .' (I, ii, 190) – where he promised to reveal his hidden and greater self to the world. In this later private scene, the playwright significantly extends the circle of confidence by one; to the theatre audience is added King Henry himself.[5] In staking his life upon his honour, Hal adds potency to his promises by reference to a set of quasi-magical acts and symbols which help to conjure up dire images of fulfilment through the enactment in blood of timeless rites. Such primitive ceremonies inform the conventional concepts of honour and loyalty with new depth and so diverge from the mainstream of acts and images of the drama as to reinforce the idea of Hal's separateness and superiority. Virginia Carr has noted the violations of the ceremonies of kingship in the Henriad, commencing with Richard II's part in the murder of Thomas Duke of Gloucester and reaching their extreme form with the murder of Richard himself in which 'we see the ultimate violation of the sanctity of kingship'.[6] If we accept this view of the causes and manifestations of the destruction of ceremony, we might recognize in Hal's highly ritualized oath and performance of his vow a gradual, but concrete, reintroduction of the substances and linked ceremonies of kingship into the state.[7]

It is in distinguishing between beneficial and harmful violence that this drama advances through mime and illusion an age-old practise of blood ritual. Ritual, René Girard reminds us, 'is nothing more than the regular exercise of "good" violence'.[8] He adds: 'If sacrifical violence is to be effective it must resemble the nonsacrificial as closely as possible.' Hal's is a promise to commit a deed of 'good' violence, and the elements of ceremony with which he intends to inform the deed only add to its ritualized nature. To Hal, his blood-covered features and the garment of blood are the necessary stage of pollution precedent to the promised regeneration. In these images, Hal imagines himself stained with Hotspur's blood and presenting himself to his father as the conqueror of his father's

– and of 'right' society's – enemy, and thus the saviour of the nation. The bloody mask is a token or a symbol of his effort on behalf of established order and will publically proclaim him as hero.

And yet it is a mask. As such, it can possess the power to disguise the wearer. Hal imagines himself not precisely bloody or blood-smeared, but as wearing bloody robes. To *wear* a garment of blood is different from bloodying one's own garments: it can mean to wear outward dress or covering which is stained with blood or to be so covered in blood as to seem to be wearing such a robe. It is likely that both meanings are intended. The latter is used as an assurance of heroic behaviour, as a part of the ritual of purification being described and, furthermore, the latter use accords more literally and immediately with the notion, two lines later, of washing away the accumulated gore on garment and face. The idea of the garment, however, as a separate robe and of the mask as an adopted guise enforces an impression of Hal as separate from the bloody object. In part, the self-imagined picture of the prince clad in his garment and mask has the effect of portraying Hal as priest or ritual slaughterer. As such, the image helps make concrete the early notion, gleaned from Hal's first soliloquy, that Prince Hal is in control of the events of this drama. Seeing himself in this functionary role, Hal is enforcing upon our attention his confident knowledge of himself as director of events. The idea of the garment is more usually associated with the softness of the priest's robes than with steely armour. The mask, too, is a part of the garb of the priest of the common imagination and known tradition who participates in the ritual.

If this is convincing – if Hal's perception of his killing of Hotspur can be accepted as an act of cleansing ('Which washed away shall scour my shame with it') – then we might also accept that Shakespeare has identified yet another crucial, if not *the* crucial difference between the hero and his heroic antagonist. The image of their encounter is variously imagined by Hal and Hotspur, and in this very variety of imagination lies the key to their essential characters. Hal shows his own control of his emotions and of his imagination. As Hotspur can be driven beyond the bounds of patience by imagination of huge exploits, so Hal remains firmly anchored within his own sensible sphere. He is the most entirely self-controlled character in the play, perhaps in the canon. In identifying the difference between Hal and Hotspur, James Calderwood notes that, 'as a future king Hal knows very well that his business is to shape history, not to be shaped by it. To Hotspur history is a fixed and final reality to which he is irrevocably committed. He has given his word, as it were; he cannot alter his role. To Hal on the other hand history is a series of roles and staged events'.[9] Hal decidedly lacks what Maynard Mark once characterized as the first quality of the tragic hero – the driving impulse to overstatement,[10] which is possessed in such impressive abundance by Hotspur. For many, Hal seems to have an overdeveloped sense of right and wrong. Equally, and equally unlike Hotspur, part of Hal's amazing political success in the play has to do with his ability to move familiarly through a variety of speech styles, each apparently selected with a view to the occasion. We have noted in the speech quoted above the impressive opening line – its straightforwardness, its rhythm, its explicit contrast with the words to which it is a response. Immediately thereafter follow seventeen lines in which Hal commits himself to fulfilment of a mission. These seventeen lines form a unit which is separate from that dramatic, assertive first line whose loneliness in the speech lends it an air of authenticity of emotion separable from the carefully contrived rhetoric of all that follows it. Within the following lines lies deep the notion of vengeance sanitized by reference to the cleansing ritual described. The idea of revenge is concentrated in the imagined destruction of an even greater Hotspur than exists – 'For every honour sitting on his helm,/Would they were multitudes, and on my head/My shames redoubled!' – and give an even sensual texture by the use and placing of the two key latinate words in the sentence, 'multitudes' and 'redoubled'. The contrast of these words and this entire section of the speech with the blunt monosyllables of line one, of the large and conventionally noble concepts of this part of the speech with the sound of outrage and grief conveyed by that first line, lends the speech the tinge of self-consciousness. What follows these seventeen lines seems to me, even more obviously, to point to a kind of cleverness in Hal that diminishes the felt rage he is trying to express: for he overlays it with metaphors too mundane to be able to carry with them the burden of moral distress by which he is ostensibly moved. I refer to the mercantile terminology by which Hal concludes his plea: 'factor', 'engross up', 'strict account', 'render every glory up', 'tear the reckoning from his heart', 'cancels all bands', 'smallest parcel', establish in this oath-taking a tone of marketplace transaction which tends to dull the burnishing imagery of ritual and heroism with which he begins. He introduces

here a new mode of speech that contrasts with the heroically extravagant promise of the culminating lines of the preceding part – 'For
the time will come/That I shall make this Northern youth exchange/
His glorious deeds for my indignities.' Norman Council observes
that the speech demonstrates the pragmatic side of the prince who
determines here 'to use Hotspur's reputation for his own gain . . . .
Hotspur's honourable reputation is useful to Hal and he means to
acquire it'.[11] The speech as a whole speaks of the sheer, even
miraculous, *competence* of the speaker. The manipulation of styles
and the variegation of tones and metaphors all denote a virtuosity
which, while commendable in itself, is somewhat vitiated when
compared to the different kind of virtuosity of Hotspur's speeches.
Finally we must note that the rhetoric of Hal's speech, in all its
variety, accomplishes its end of gaining the king's good opinion. In
this sense, of course, the speech is bound to be suspect, since the
whole is motivated by a desire or need of the prince to persuade the
king, his powerful father, of his loyalty. And there must be satis-
faction for Hal and his partisans in Henry's clear change of heart,
conveyed by his confident assertion, 'A hundred thousand rebels
die in this' (III, ii, 160).

   All theatre audiences are accustomed to seeing people tempor-
arily transformed into other people for the duration of the play.
Audiences of and participants in rituals, however, see the process
and function of ritual as a means to permanent transformation of a
person into, essentially, another person – a boy becomes a man, a
girl a woman, a man a priest. Shakespeare critics have been reasonably united in recognizing the transformation of Hal from wayward
boyhood to manhood after this speech; Harold Jenkins, for
example, sees this exchange between father and son as the 'nodal
point' of the play.[12] One may go further, I believe, in recognizing
the transformation of Hal as being the transformation of the protagonist of the play into a hero – and one may identify the moment of
transformation as the first line of this speech. To recognize the
transformation as made permanent by virtue of a ritualized oath-
taking has the effect of strengthening and universalizing the nature
and extent of the change and, hence, of anticipating with certainty,
the triumph of this hero in a drama which seems to depend frequently upon the formal modes of myth.

   I say 'this hero' because the uniqueness of 1 *Henry IV* resides very
largely in the fact that this is a play with two heroes, each of whom
stands at the centre of a world which has been conceived in oppo-

sition to that of the other. Those worlds are separately defined units of place and ideology which cannot coexist; for their separate existences are partially defined by the pledge of each to destroy the other. The ideologies for which the two heroes stand are at bottom the same – those of power and control.

The encounter between them is the occasion of the play's greatest emotional intensity. The moment has been predicted, vaunted, hoped for by participants and heroes alike. The privacy of the confrontation – interrupted briefly by Douglas and Falstaff – does not in any sense diminish the timeless ritual with which it is informed. We note the common expressions of recognition and identification, whose tone of defiance maintains the note of hostility necessary to such life-and-death meetings as these. And we note the nearly compulsive need of each hero to articulate to the other his sense of the meaning of the moment. The form of the expression of each is remarkable: Hal's chivalry and Hotspur's haste are appropriate symbolic denotations of each as he is given the opportunity to express his sense of the significance of the moment, demonstrating that he knows, as his opposite knows, that for one of them it is a last encounter. It is this awareness of finality that endues the moment with solemnity and the ritual with its form – that of a last accounting in the dazzling light of a certain death to follow.

The encounter, when if finally comes, is preceded by a provocative ritual of boasting in which each of the combatants – almost as if to rediscover the basis of his hatred of the other – recalls the very spirit of his own animosity. In Hal's recollection of the Ptolemaic principle that 'Two stars keep not their motion in one sphere' (V, iv, 64) he falls back upon the natural law, resistance to whose principles he has begun to abandon since his vow to the king. And indeed it is in obedience to the laws of nature that Hal has ritually dedicated himself. Hotspur's over-weening vanity makes him hark back, compulsively almost, to the lust for greatness that dooms him. But it is when Hal, oddly and mockingly, borrows Hotspur's own demotic language and metaphors of violent action, that the Northern youth is finally left without images and must act:

> Prince.   I'll make it greater ere I part from thee,
> And all the budding honours on thy crest
> I'll crop to make a garland for my head.

Hotspur.   I can no longer brook thy vanities.

(V, iv, 79–4)

Hal's words, his image of Hotspur's 'budding' honours, suggest to his adversary that those honours are not yet full-grown, not really the honours of an adult hero. His threat to 'crop' them from his crest contains an insulting contempt: to crop, according to the *OED*, is 'to poll or to lop off'. The term, in other words carries all the easy arrogance of a simple, almost casual, single deadly blow. In Hal's brilliantly infuriating image we and, more important, Hotspur are presented with the image of Hotspur as an unresisting plant and the prince as a carefree courtier in search of 'a garland for [his] head'. Hotspur's single line of reply is, thus, reasonably one of powerful anger: his only possible reply to Hal's vanities is the testing action of combat.

Of the dying Hotspur, George Hibbard has written that he 'eventually becomes capable of seeing all human endeavour, including his own, in relation to the great abstract ideas of time and eternity, and voices this vision of things in the moving lines he utters at his end'.[13] This observation in part explains the tragic element of this character in the coalescence of his comic and tragic selves into mutually supporting images of comedy and tragedy whose very extremism lends intensity to the character. There is tragedy, too, in the dying man's sheer magnificent truth to himself, to what he is and has ever been; 'I better brook the loss of brittle life/Than those proud titles thou has won of me', comes not from the large heart of the tragic vision but from the authentic, single, separate self of Harry Hotspur, uniquely and eternally apart. That difference from his fellows, from all other heroes, is gloriously captured in the penultimate realization that the instrument by which he has lived, by which his life and character have been defined, has been stilled – 'the cold hand of death/Lies on my tongue'. Hotspur, whose eloquence has elevated him, is unimaginable in a silent state, and Shakespeare, knowing the absolute truth of this for the character and the audience, rivets all attention upon the death of his hero's speech. Thus does silence become synonymous with tragedy.

The prolonged antagonism of Hal and Hotspur has no obviously alternative outcome to this final violent conflict. And in the conflict itself we can discern the fact that the physical closeness of the antagonists is a metaphor for a larger issue evident in the spectacle. That, as the two have been driven gradually closer through the play, so have they become with the subtle aid of ritual, more and more alike until, in the moments of and those immediately after, the fatal fight, they are almost images of each other. So utterly does violence dominate mimetic and dramatic action that it can result in the obliteration of individuality. During the violent encounter differences between combatants tend to evanesce: the violence itself is the correlative by which individuals are connected as their whole selves are absorbed by physical contention. Hal and Hotspur do not speak during their fight and thus are transformed by their attempts to kill each other into a single unit of dramatic action – the differences between them disappear; their personalities meld. And, indeed, it would seem that in killing Hotspur, and through the combat itself, Hal has absorbed something of his opponent's vital essence. There is an indication, in his tribute to the fallen hero, of love and something, too, of the generosity of soul which is Hotspur's hallmark.

> Prince.   For worms, brave Percy. Fare thee well, great heart!
> Ill-weav'd ambition, how much art thou shrunk!
> When that this body did contain a spirit,
> A kingdom for it was too small a bound;
> But now two paces of the vilest earth
> Is room enough: this earth that bears thee dead
> Bears not alive so stout a gentleman.
> If thou wert sensible of courtesy,
> I should not make so dear a show of zeal;
> But let my favours hide thy mangled face,
> And, even in thy behalf, I'll thank myself
> For doing these rites of tenderness.
> Adieu, and take thy praise with thee to heaven!
> Thy ignominy sleep with thee in the grave,
> But not remember'd in thy epitaph!

> (V, iv, 86–100)

The ritualistic element of the speech takes the form of a loving tribute to the fallen hero and an action of passing symbolic import. Hal, Herbert Hartman has convincingly argued, disengages his own royal plumes from his helmet to shroud the face of his dead rival.[14] These plumes are equivalent to Hotspur's 'budding honours' so contemptuously referred to by the prince at the commencement of the encounter. If we can suppose Hal actually to have fulfilled his threat and, as the text allows, to have cropped Hotspur's plumes, then surely the removal of his own plumes and the act of placing them upon the face of the beloved enemy is a gesture of weight. In the purest sense of the phrase, Hal *identifies with* Hotspur, and that identification is given a poignant depth by the ritualistic means through which it is achieved.

In other ways the speech contains evidence of this identification which seems so much stronger than sympathy. By concluding Hotspur's dying speech Hal has appropriated to himself something of the power of his rival's speech; he has almost literally absorbed his last breath. Despite the obviousness of the tendency of Hotspur's last words, Hal's mere capacity to utter them cements the identification.

Ten lines later, concomitantly with his 'rites of tenderness', Prince Hal bends over the body of Hotspur to lay his favours on the soldier's face. In so doing he closes once again – and for only the second time in the drama – the physical space between them as he touches his erstwhile adversary. Hal thus bathes his own favours which clearly have immensely strong symbolic, even religious, meaning for him – in the blood of Harry Hotspur. And thus, ironically, does Hotspur acquire a mask soaked in his own blood *and* the blood of the prince. For, as Hal performs his act of homage, we are powerfully reminded of his solemn oath to the king to 'stain my favours in a bloody mask'. In the mingling of the blood of Prince Hal and Harry Hotspur is the fusion of their two souls symbolically extended. The words by which Hal accompanies his gesture complete the connection: 'And even in thy behalf I'll thank myself . . .' The pronouns of that line, by their self-conscious interplay, bind their subjects ever more firmly to each other. As well, history furnished Shakespeare with one additional means by which the two characters are made to merge; that is, of course, the unforgettable fact that they have the same Christian name.

The degradation of honour and courage which Falstaff's presence offers the scene has often been discussed. One is reminded of Falstaff's capacity for sheer bestiality as he defiles the body lying near him; a capacity made more real, perhaps, by the use to which he subsequently puts the newly mangled corpse. As an ironic travesty, the gesture has an axiomatic dramatic function in keeping with the structure of parody running through the drama. However, less obvious – aside from the action's merely narrative purpose – is the reason for the action in relation, not to the scheme or structure of the drama but, precisely, to the Prince's killing of Hotspur.

A nation in a state of civil war is one in which law has failed to create or maintain order. And so it is beyond the law that the state must seek the means of stability. The means are often those of repression, which always carries the threat of resistance. Thus do the two opposing forces of tyranny and resistance to tyranny promise the fruition of actual conflict. Societies suffering repression can explode in violence which is artistically expressed as an image of the artist's political prejudice. As the violent riots of *Henry VI* are devoid of the seeds of social order, in *1 Henry IV* the conflict and its hero are presented so as to emphasize a socially beneficial outcome. Here, the blood that is shed fulfills the requirements of blood rituals. It is, one might say, 'clean' blood resulting from what René Girard has called 'good' acts of violence.[15] That is, it is blood which has been shed for the larger advantage of the national welfare. And as we look back at the blood imagery related to the Hal/Hotspur conflict, it becomes clear that Hotspur's blood has been represented as that of the sacrificial creature whose death will redeem his world, and into whose life and person are concentrated the rage, anxiety, and fear of a threatened nation. His death, then, sometimes regarded as tragic, is also utterly necessary for the continuation of the nation. Dover Wilson regards it as a favourable feature of Hal's character that his 'epitaph on Hotspur contains not a word of triumph',[16] and perhaps he is right. But, for Shakespeare and his audience, more significant, perhaps, is the fact that Hotspur's greatness was very nearly sufficient unto his purposes: the world was almost overturned, and with it the reign of the regicide Henry IV. Hal's presence here naturally palliates the thought, since Hal is the successor to the throne of the tyrant and, just as surely, the golden hero of the drama.

At his death and because of it, Hotspur is transformed into a hero of tragic magnitude. Thus, when Falstaff rises and hacks at his corpse, he commits a direct assault upon the sanctity of the ritual that has just been performed. His act suddenly infuses the scene with uncleanness by an almost casual reversal of the ritual that has just passed. The return to life of Falstaff is no miracle, but a rather sour joke, made somewhat sourer by the attitude of shallow boasting which accompanies it. The return to prose, to a disordered unrhythmic speech which breathes selfish relief and opportunism is a wicked riposte to Hal. But the physical attack on Hotspur' corpse is a *crime* against the ethos of heroism to which the princ and, in a dramatic sense, the nation have been committed. Falstaff'. act is a negation and a degradation of the cleansing by blood. An yet the repeated exposure to violence can inure us to it. While w are indeed shocked by the callous treatment of Hotspur's corpse the very brutality of that treatment and its very extensivenes gradually accustom us to the shocking fact that a slain hero is bein dragged around like a side of beef. The corpse of Hotspur graduall becomes the focus not merely of Falstaff's opportunism, but of grotesque, huge, successful joke – 'one of the best jokes in th whole drama'[17] upon whose point is balanced the question of ritua purification. Yet Falstaff's imitative act of violence rebounds upor himself: any doubts as to his locus in the moral scheme of the pla are vividly resolved by his disruption of the cycle of the ritual. Th emphatic terminus implied by Hal's parting words is crassl mocked by Falstaff rising up. The act of cutting Percy's thigh i represented as antithetical to Hal's death-fight with Percy: as th fight was a lucid example of the purifying violence seen only ir drama and ritual, so the attack on the corpse affirmed the value o the rite by its implied but debased reenactment of the encounter.

Hal, Hotspur, and Falstaff are, then, related through ritual, both in itself and as depicted through the dark glass of parody and travesty. Furthermore, it is through ritual that they are connected tc their world in the play's intensest moments. To call Falstaff's imper sonation of Hal's father in the tavern scene a parody is to diminish the force of a scene in which a youth enacts one of the deepes universal desires of man as he overthrows his tyrannical father. The scene of oath-taking, discussed earlier, is a conscious, deliberate and calculated retraction of the desires enacted in the tavern. A such, it is either utterly false or it is the heroic conquest of reasor and responsibility – that is, social pressure and expectation – ove the urging of the unconscious mind – that is, individual nature. It i thus profitable to see the tavern ritual and its climactic, if soft spoken, conclusion ('I do, I will' [II, iv, 475]) as a ritual of exorcism by which Prince Hal, through the contrived dramatization of hi innermost promptings, rids himself of the demons of his deepes desires. As J. I. M. Stewart has argued with reference to the rejec tion of Falstaff: Hal, 'by a displacement common enough in th

·volution of a ritual, kills Falstaff instead of killing the king, his
ather'.[18]

Hotspur, on the other hand, does not grow or change. From first
o last his purpose is to gain glory and renown. Even at his death, it
s to his honours that he refers as having been more dearly won of
iim than his life. His sheer consistency makes him an apt victim in
he cruel drama of ritual sacrifice. A Hotspur who can go to his
1eath proclaiming the value of a moral system which is by its nature
·xclusive of the vast world from which it derives, cannot be the hero
vho heals the world. His presence nearly always provides discor-
1ancy, charming and witty though it may be. He is the heart of the
vhirlwind that rages through the nation, and it is this heart that
nust be stilled for the sake of peace. In short, as with other tragic
:haracters, it is Hotspur's death alone that can heal the world.

3 *Measure for Measure* and the Drama of Pornography

In its illumination of the relation that exists between power and sexuality *Measure for Measure* provides a vision of the pornographic mind. Pornography, like most forms of eroticism, exists within the individual mind as it relates to a sexual object outside itself. Unlike most forms of eroticism, pornography is contingent upon the outside object being ultimately submissive to the originating, conceptualizing self. That is, pornography takes its form from the idea of total control of an imagined other. Thus pornography, like many forms of eroticism is fantastic, since it depends upon the submission of the 'other' to the originating self in a wholly impossible way. The other becomes merely a compliant element of the self, losing its individuality, its independence, its identity entirely in the initiating mind. In this sense, it is unreal. Thus while, conceivably, pornographic desires may be physically enacted, they can never be wholly satisfying because that element of absorption into the initiating self can never be complete or demonstrable. It is surely this factor of the pornographic mind being ultimately insatiable that accounts for the varieties and degrees of debasement that constitutes pornography. For the debasement is the purest form of the attempt to demonstrate and assert the existence and the extent of control of the originating mind over that other.

In *Measure for Measure* Shakespeare provides a drama of pornographic desire. The likeness of Angelo and Isabella is thoroughly discussed in the literature about the play. But their unlikeness is the key to the mind of Angelo and the drama of desire that occurs between them. Criticism of the sexual aspect of the play is curious and interesting. On the one hand, critics have noted, frequently with great perspicacity, the presence of sexual tension within Angelo and Isabella individually, and in doing so have enforced the notion of their likeness to each other which Shakespeare clearly encourages us to see. What is less often pointed out, perhaps because it is obvious and perhaps because critics are themselves prone to pressures of gender, is that while the whole focus of Angelo's desire is Isabella and his fantasy the use and manipulation of her, the focus of Isabella's desire is no other person. Her words denoting desire include no other. They are classically auto-erotic. And in this depiction of the separate incompatible ideas of eroticism in the minds of his two protagonists, Shakespeare has sharply delineated the distinction between the erotic and the pornographic. To disinclude in Isabella's eroticism any other is boldly and unambiguously to have asserted her innocence and anticipated the cruel isolation to which she is subjected in her last moments as she contemplates marriage. Having sought more strict restraints upon herself in the beginning, she appears to have found them in the total submission of an apparently unwilling self in the end. She seems in the last scene to have found her nemesis in fulfilling for the Duke the requirements of Angelo's desires, submitting her body, her chastity, that gift she values more than life itself, to a man.

The plot of this play, as Ralph Berry has noted, 'is based to a degree not found elsewhere in the canon on the *fact* of the sexual act'.[1] Claudio's crime is the actual and symbolic fact to which every character in the play is compelled to relate, and in this relation and through this relation are the many selves of the drama exposed. As L. C. Knights has pointed out, it is Claudio 'who stands between the two extremes – who seems to spring from the feelings at war with themselves, and it is considering the nature of his offense that one feels the most perplexity'.[2] The Duke, Escalus, Mistress Overdone, Pompey Bum, and of course Lucio, Angelo, and Isabella all take note of the crime and in so doing expose an essential part of themselves. They are vitally connected to the heart of the play precisely by their acknowledgement of the existence of Claudio. As Shakespeare's romantic comedies are sometimes said to contain and revolve around the varieties of love and to present at many levels its experience, so *Measure for Measure* centres upon the sexual act with a concreteness not possible in love comedy where a kind of abstractness necessarily obtains. Sex, however, is a satiable, physical need. As such it has been transformed into a commodity in this marketplace of Vienna. It can be bought and stolen by men: it has become an item of transaction both willing and unwilling, and it has been appropriated by the power structure of the state as an agent of law enforcement. For while morality, like love, is unenforceable, sex in this society of Vienna – as in most societies – has come to stand for, to symbolize, both love and morality as their concrete and physical manifestation. The restoration of sex to the marriage bed at the end of the drama has the effect, first of all, of placing it once more into the confines of a system of order and under a paternal or, even, patriarchal control. That is, the relegitimization of sex results in the restoration of the bourgeois morality whose endangerment is the motive for the Duke's departure. Shakespeare's object in the drama has been to show the relation of the individuals of the society to the fact of sexual life and to demonstrate the extremes of behaviour to which sex is capable of controlling and driving men and women. A by-product of this objective is the demonstration that sex is capable of being transformed into an object of legal and illegal transaction, and that, in the interests of a partriarchal order, it can be controlled.[3]

While sex is indeed the central fact of the play, its connection with love is also expressed. What we might find somewhat remarkable is how very seldom it is expressed. Of the twenty nine uses in *Measure for Measure* of the word love I can find only one in which the lover speaks objectively and factually about his own love of the woman he loves. Significantly and ironically that single usage of the word is Claudio's, when in Act I, scene ii, line 152, he observes to Lucio, 'we thought it meet to hide our love/Till time had made them for us'. Juliet in Act II, ii, line 40, on hearing of Claudio's imminent death cries, 'O injurious love,/That respites me a life whose very comfort/Is still a dying horror.' Elsewhere in the play the word is used in very different contexts, none of them expressing a 'normal' felt love relation of a man to a woman. There is the Duke talking of the love of his subjects, and his love of them. He speaks of Mariana's love of Angelo and in the last scene rather amazingly orders or enjoins Angelo to love Mariana. There is Angelo's use of the word in reference to Isabella. There is divine love. But, aside from Claudio's remark that he loved Juliet and Juliet's apostrophe to love, the idea of love receives a decidedly unromantic treatment.

Love in action, then, is not a common sight in this play. Claudio and Juliet who seem to love each other are not seen together. However, there is an example of love shown: it is that of Lucio to Claudio. This relationship needs to be examined because, as a love relationship, it is quite different and infinitely more hopeful in its possibilities than the pornographic distortion of love which Angelo expresses in his relating to Isabella. Lucio's view of the crime, first of all, is utterly subversive of the law. And perhaps it is this that makes him an object of the duke's hatred. To him what Claudio has done or committed may go under many names, but crime is not one of them. He refuses from start to finish to acknowledge that Claudio has endangered social order. To him the problem admits of a simple and clear solution; that is, not to label sex criminal; to do so is to violate common sense. In political terms this is simply to say that the law is a bad law and it is by believing this that the believer becomes a threat to social order. Lucio's feeling for Claudio's plight is humane and sympathetic, and his love of Claudio inspires him, alone amongst Claudio's friends, to act to save him. His view of sex, too liberal for some and too male chauvinist for others, is nevertheless morally clear, and, if we consider the grotesque farce that is made of lawful intercourse at the end of the drama, we might find ourselves drawn instead to Lucio's perhaps gross but not brutal alternative.

Angelo and Isabella, initially repelled by Claudio's act of fornication are slowly drawn towards it by circumstance and a species of revulsion that seems a negative desire. The act around which they concentrate so much of their energy and whose consequences fill their lives with new meaning and purpose takes on for each of these protagonists, powerful overtones. It is the living fact of vice and comes to symbolize the very essence of evil. As it comes thus to represent a central repugnant fact in each of their lives separately and individually, so the image of sexuality represents the correlative force to which each relates his and her own sense of sexual identity. For it is to this central act that each must refer as a means of clarifying his own moral and emotional perspectives on society and self. To all but Angelo and Isabella there is a forgiveable naturalness about Claudio's act, and only these two are unable to identify with Claudio. Angelo and Isabella, however, have consciously rejected the paths of the ordinary and natural. But though their rejection of or aversion from nature and its synonym, sex, makes them unusual, it also makes them more complexly human.

In portraying the sexual complexity of Isabella, Shakespeare has stressed her impulse towards isolation from the world. Thus her lonely and independent eroticism stands as a symbol of the separating unsocial self seeking fulfillment without reference to the world to which it is bound. Not content merely to leave society for the company of nuns, Isabella in the convent wishes even to abjure the company of the sisterhood: 'I speak not as desiring more,/But

rather wishing a more strict restraint/Upon the sisterhood . . .' (I
iv, 3–5). Between the thought contained and suppressed in this
expression and that of the profoundly erotic language of crisis there
is a strong link.

> . . . were I under the terms of death,
> Th'impression of keen whips I'd wear as rubies,
> And strip myself to death as to a bed
> That longing have been sick for, ere I'd yield
> My body up to shame

> (II, iv, 100–4)

Here the idea of restraint is taken to an extreme. Where in the earlier
speech she refers to the idea of restraint as mere restriction of
physical movement, as a restriction upon the society she is permitted to keep, upon the words she is permitted to utter, upon the
humanity she is to be exposed to, in this heartfelt utterance the idea
of restraint is made synonymous with heroic challenge, a restraint
of life, a restraint to death.[4] The tangible, measureable challenge to
abide by the rules of the sisterhood takes on the fervid force of
martyrdom. For in the latter speech the compulsions are beyond the
mere adherence to rule, but rather they are self-enforced, embody-
ing an act of pure will whereby the speaker chooses a painful death,
an end which no rule demands however severe the life it may
impose upon its adherents. The eroticism of the speech lies largely
in its passionate embrace of physical anguish, in its association of
death with physical sensation, and in its refulgent, almost extra-
vagantly vivid images of the anguish of martyrdom. The idea of
yielding up her body elicits a dark and powerful excitement in
Isabella, the excitement made pure by the climax of death. The
image excites her because of its pure submission to herself. Thus
Isabella's desire for restraint, for seclusion from society, finds a
kind of apotheosis in a desire for death. Her passion, by which this
speech is carried, bespeaks not merely an alternative to Angelo's
proposal of sexual surrender, instead it argues a hunger for a physical – synonymous in this play with sexual – sensation which is so
great that only death can provide it. If Angelo is aroused by this
image it is because the idea which Isabella here gives of her deepest
self and most deeply concealed desire is in conformity with a
certain species of male desire for female debasement. In its exclu-

sion of another – consistent in this sense with the first wish for restraint – the speech inspires in Angelo a desire to nullify the notion of sexual independence by his own domination of the speaker. The image is sexually exciting in that it includes a reference to Isabella stripped to a bed yet alone; she is imagined as physically and sexually anguished, yet she is independent. The male desire, shared perhaps by the author of this fantasy, is drawn to the image because it is so bluntly excluded from it.

Above all, the auto-eroticism of this speech is an assertion of the independence of the self. The image indicates a desire for freedom from the fetters that make submission to masculine authority normal, necessary, and inevitable in this social world. No man in the play does not want Isabella to submit her will to his, in which pattern of sexual behaviour she comes to be regarded as a cypher in her dealings with men. As the play progresses that process of the subjugation of Isabella to the men she encounters becomes increasingly evident and predictable. Isabella's life contains no serenity: it consists of one after another encounter with male authority and the external and internal conflicts and challenges which these encounters create. The central conflict with Angelo strikes at the very core of the gender issue around which the play revolves by its direct and unambiguous concern with the sexuality of the characters involved. Angelo's discovery of his sexuality necessarily involves Isabella in the matter of sexuality, both his own, as the man attracted to her, and consequently her own.

As Isabella has idealized femaleness as coincident with chastity, so Angelo perceives that his own chasteness of temper makes him a saint (II, ii, 180). That is, in the minds of these two characters, male and female perfectibility are bound up with sexual chastity. The undoubted arrogance of each of them derives from the fact in one case and the likelihood in the other that the practise of celibacy comes easily. The witty denigrations of Angelo's physical constitution are all accurate up until the point of his encounter with Isabella. Thus Angelo and Isabella's perceptions of self, conditioned as they must be by contrasts between themselves and the differently inclined community, possess a built-in assurance of their superiority in the important regard of sexuality. That is, they live in a society which condemns the very sexuality it freely practises; Angelo and Isabella find themselves able to condemn sexuality without needing to practise it.

Isabella's encounter with Angelo demands an act of heroic self

assertion as she compels herself to overcome natural diffidence.
Her first effort at pleading for her brother, which Lucio describes as
being 'too cold' (II, ii, 56) is less 'cold' than timid in the face of
masculine authority represented by the deputy. The feebleness of
that first fledgeling effort to persuade Angelo derives from an
adherence to the public dictates of her and Angelo's publically
recognized social and sexual roles. Initially she is unable to recognize in the judge the man beneath the robes. She sees him as the
embodiment of Justice itself and as a consequence relates her suit
not to the man she addresses but rather to the figure he stands for.
She meets Angelo with 'I am a woeful suitor to your honour;/Please
but your honour hear me' (II, ii, 27–8). And prepares to part from
him with another phrase that asserts his rightful guardianship over
social behaviour; 'O just but severe law!/I had a brother, then:
heaven keep your honour' (II, ii, 42–3). While the references to
Angelo's 'honour' are undoubtedly ironic they also reflect,
however, Isabella's spontaneous awareness of the sexual and social
distance between herself and Angelo. Her suit seems to include
here a desire to establish her own moral credentials with authority
quite as much as to fulfil her mission. Her first speech while it
reflects confusion in its self-consciously introverted and inverted
clauses is quite specifically about herself. Isabella is almost syco-
phantic towards the judge as she aligns herself with him in expressing agreement with his reprobation of the crime.

> There is a vice that most I do abhor,
> And most desire should meet the blow of justice;
> For which I would not plead, but that I must;
> For which I must not plead but that I am
> At war 'twixt will and will not.

> (II, ii, 29–33)

The part of Isabella that 'would not plead' and 'must not plead' is
the public woman's part. Social propriety and religious cause
demand conformity with social justice and religious condemnation. The part that must and *is,* is the simply eloquent private
female self, the other half of Isabella. It is this half that ultimately
triumphs over the promptings of Isabella's public self and which
succeeds in penetrating Angelo's carapace. And to Lucio must go
the credit for providing by his prompting the impetus that forces

Isabella to permit that private self to the surface of her austere and rigorously controlled public self. The energy of the encounter that follows takes its moral and emotional power from Isabella's inspiration. She, as Philip Edwards has said, 'has the fire and ice of her faith and convictions to guide her'.[5] That force seems to flow from the pristine eloquence of the savagely simple single question which she, turning from her proposed departure, directs at Angelo: 'Must he needs die?' (II, ii, 48).

The question revives the human tragedy which Angelo has initiated. It recalls to the consciousness of Isabella the single factor almost forgotten by her in her public reprehension of the vice of fornication – it recalls the living fact of Claudio and his suffering. In the great debate which follows she slips with passionate skill between the abstract moral issues and the immediate personal matter which inspires her eloquence. From the fervid language of religious conviction she plucks the personal and individual agony which makes it relevant. Again and again Isabella forces Angelo to face the human consequence of his tyranny. Underlying her stunning rhetoric is the simple image of the three actors in this preventable tragedy, *I, thou,* and *he*. By her relentless appeals to Angelo's humanity and individuality Isabella succeeds in slowly breaking through the impersonal face of justice to pierce the man beneath. His determined objectivity is shaken by the appeal for pity to him directly and not to the law which he keeps invoking as a protection for himself. To Angelo's iron statement, 'The law hath not been dead, though it hath slept . . .' (II, ii, 91). Isabella responds in a direct assault upon the man who stands behind it, 'Yet show some pity' (II, ii, 100).

And here at last, Angelo himself steps forth, separate from his mask of public office. 'I show it most of all when I show justice:/For then I pity those I do not know' (II, ii, 101–2). He acknowledges his own role in the drama, his own responsibility for the exercise of power. The same man who has asserted 'It is the law not I condemn your brother' (II, ii, 80) is now forced to acknowledge a human self that stands behind the law. The repeated use of the first person in the two lines, so untypical of Angelo's speech suggests the developing identification of the man with his public role. The perhaps unconscious involvement of his private self with his formal self leads to a long silence in which he seems to be struggling with the promptings of the private. His question to Isabella, 'Why do you put these sayings upon me?' (II, ii, 134) possesses a quality of uncertainty quite unlike the decisive righteousness of the earlier lines where he is quick to pronounce his authority. The aside he speaks serves strongly to reinforce that newly hesitant mode that his private self has uncovered. And thus, in the most private possible terms, Angelo shows that he himself has been reduced to the scale of ordinary humanity by his reduction of the elements of the argument to a simple equation of *she* and *I*: 'She speaks, and 'tis such sense/That my sense breeds with it' (II, ii, 142–3). The sexual connotations of 'breeds', which have been noted by William Empson[6] are indicators of the incipient crisis of sexual identity which cause Angelo's downfall. He is at the brink of the confrontation with himself by which he is brought to the state of being, like Shylock and Malvolio, simultaneously the villain and the victim of the drama.

Towards the end of the encounter, a disturbed Angelo, in imitation of Isabella earlier, turns to leave. Like Isabella, he is diverted from that purpose by a fatal exhortation. This time it is Isabella pleadingly recalling him to the path of mercy in justice. The form of this recall has the effect upon Angelo of a profound sexual titillation. He turns and returns to hear the chilling anti-sexual (to him) sound of the word 'bribe'. 'How! Bribe me?' (II, ii, 147). His surprise denotes the potential for a drastic and immediate reversal of the sexual tide that has begun to swell in him. And then, with a devastating rhetorical blow Isabella re-reverses even more powerfully this passionately burgeoning sexuality by striking with almost uncanny accuracy at Angelo's weakness. She paints with her words a picture of the very thing which causes him to disintegrate – a picture of mysterious, submissive, and ethereal maidens like herself all concentrating their most spiritual thoughts upon him. Isabella becomes his most private sexual self as she fleshes out for him, in hitherto unimagined detail, the fantasy of himself most certain to undo him. While the Duke has offered Angelo a worldly power, Isabella offers what must surely be seen as an even greater temptation for one of Angelo's bent, a bribe of

> true prayers,
> That shall be up at heaven and enter there
> Ere sunrise: prayers from preserved souls,
> From fasting maids, whose minds are dedicate
> To nothing temporal.

> (II, ii, 152–6)

At this moment, the distance that the two have come from Claudio and his plight is great indeed. Isabella, as Mary Lascelles has said, is only dimly mindful of her brother himself; rather, in a sense, she is pleading for all mankind.[7] While Angelo concentrates his whole attention inward upon this newly awakened sense he recognizes almost no outward world but that which contains himself and this austere and provocative novice. In acknowledging the urging of a hitherto dormant physical self he is facing the fact and meaning of his masculinity. Until now, being a man for Angelo has meant the requisite fulfilment of an almost purely social function – his treatment of Mariana indicates not so much a harshly immoral temperament as a business-like and indifferent regard for sex roles. But the sudden introduction to his conscious mind of the vital sexual self is devastating for Angelo's self-awareness. The edifice of abstinent and austere masculine authority, the work of a lifetime in creating, crumbles to dust in the face of sensual awakening – 'this virtuous maid/Subdues me quite' (II, ii, 185–6). It is Angelo's tragedy compulsively to confuse masculinity with corruption. It appears that Angelo's feelings for Isabella are, equally with lust, the feelings of love – an inclination, as so frequently in Shakespeare, to be with the adored object, to bask in her/his sight, to 'desire to hear her speak again . . ./And feast upon her eyes . . .' (II, ii, 178–9). He surely suspects his own emotions, but as he begins to articulate them, they seem to savour of love as well as lust. Such, however, is Angelo's fear of or disdain for sexual feelings of any kind that it is logical for him to confuse the two sensations.

To Angelo, because of who and what he is, there can be no distinction between the erotic and pornographic urges or between love and lust. As both a man and a judge, his power over Isabella is immense; the fact that she has emphasized this aspect of their relationship by her description of virgins praying as much to him as for him only strengthens his awareness of the inequality between them. His 'love' of Isabella – as he calls it – he can depict only as foul, corrupt, and rotten because it stems from an inner and spontaneous sexual self which has not, till now, formed a part of his carefully cultivated being. And yet we must note the differences Angelo enunciates between his physical reaction to Isabella and his judgement of this reaction. We note him assert that he loves her and desires again to hear her voice and look into her eyes. His whole being is subdued by her. He judges these feelings as foul desires, corrupt and evil. His question, 'Shall we desire to raze the sanctuary/And pitch our evils there?' (II, ii, 171–2) speaks directly to an awareness of his power over Isabella, man's power over woman. Though his desire is evil, it is impelled by the knowledge of his strength and her weakness – his power to hurt and hers to be hurt. While he can recognize the moral catastrophe implied by his own thoughts, he sees the whole situation in terms of violent conquest – 'to raze the sanctuary/And pitch our [men's] evils there [upon women's helplessness]' (II, ii, 170–1). Angelo's confusion in this speech, at this crisis of identity is made manifest by a fragmentation of himself evident in his use of personal pronouns. He is *I*, *we*, and *our*, and perhaps most tellingly, he is the distanced separated *thou*, as he attempts to place the erring side of himself in relation to Angelo, the judge:

> Can it be
> That modesty may more betray our sense
> Than woman's lightness: Having waste ground enough,
> Shall we desire to raze the sanctuary
> And pitch our evils there? O fie, fie, fie!
> What dost thou, or what art thou, Angelo?
> Dost thou desire her foully for those things
> That make her good?

> (II, ii, 168–72)

The fragmentation, made explicit in Angelo's next soliloquy, is brought to a resolution on a note of fear. Angelo's farewell to his innocence is powerfully reminiscent of those farewells to their former selves of so many of Shakespeare's tragic heroes. In a moment of blinding clarity Angelo suddenly knows that he and his world are undone. That perfectly formed and nurtured self, the compound of probity and gravity, gives way before a force greater than itself, a force by which 'tongue' and 'invention' are split asunder.

> O place, O form,
> How often dost thou with thy case, thy habit,
> Wrench awe from fools, and tie the wiser souls
> To thy false seeming.

> (II, iv, 12–5)

The apostrophe strikes a note almost of mourning for that lost former self now known to have been a contrivance. 'Blood, thou art blood' (II, iv, 15) is more than a statement of acceptance of the inevitable. With that single, simple phrase Angelo resolves his crisis in a consciously terrible obedience to the power he has loathed and avoided his whole life. The phrase commands attention to the extent of the reversal of the entire direction of this tragically riven individual mind as it faces and succumbs to evil. Angelo does much more than surrender here: in the sentence that follows, yet another crucial moment in the drama, Angelo embraces a power he knows to be wicked with the same ardour and excitement with which he formerly sought virtue and gravity. 'Let's write good angel on the devil's horn –/'Tis not the devil's crest' (II, iv, 16–17) is an eager plunge into evil. For who is the 'us' of 'Let's' if not all of *man*kind of whom Angelo now, for the first time, sees himself as one? Thus does Angelo in this soliloquy with its multiplicity of personae find a natural equilibrium and, even, a release in his identification with other men.

Such identification, normal for all other men in the drama, remains for Angelo an act of conscious will. There is a perverse heroism in his willingness to destroy the edifice of sanctity which he has made of his life. For he does not merely stand back and watch his ideals collapse, his goodness die; rather, having seen a new light, he tears them down with his own hands. While sexual excitement shakes him profoundly he is quickly able to recognize it as such, perplexed by its absoluteness and his powerlessness in the face of it:

> O heavens,
> Why does my blood thus muster to my heart,
> Making both it unable for itself
> And dispossessing all my other parts
> Of necessary fitness?

> (II, iv, 19–23)

But the plummet into sexual tyranny is ordained by the conscious discovery of a new self and made inevitable by the fact of who and what Angelo is. Wielding immense power over Isabella, whom he loves, possessed by the desire to conquer her sexually – to 'raze the sanctuary' – and almost ritually dedicated to follow the commands

of his blood, Angelo is driven by unavoidable logic to seek fulfillment through the exercise of that power. Evident in Angelo's
plunge into sexual life is the synonymity of power and masculinity.
His abuse of that power is merely an extreme example of the uses to
which it is put by men whose unequal relation to women make of
their ascendancy a fragile and potentially dangerous matter. The
Duke's marriage proposals, while they undoubtedly lack the brutality of Angelo's use of this power, speak, nonetheless clearly of
the same tyranny of gender. Angelo puts the question into its
clearest and most destructive context when he places the dreadful
alternative before Isabella:

> Fit thy consent to my sharp appetite;
> Lay by all nicety and prolixious blushes
> That banish what they sue for. Redeem thy brother
> By yielding up thy body to my will;
> Or else he must not only die the death,
> But thy unkindness shall his death draw out
> To ling'ring sufferance.

> (II, iv, 160–6)

The threat precisely draws the distinction between male and female
and concomitantly between authority and suppliant. In the
warning that Claudio is to be tortured as well, Angelo discovers the
illimitability of pornography in its invariable correspondence of
brutality and sexuality. Erotic pleasure for the power-monger is
reached through the application of power and the consequent elici-
tation of pain. Sexuality has everything to do with strength dominating weakness, the free will controlling the unfree. Pornography
becomes significant – exists – not in the desire – for there is almost
no one without pornographic desire – but in the act. Angelo's threat
to kill and torture Isabella's brother is an *act* of pornographic
enormity wherein are enacted the united urges of the exercise of
absolute power and absolute sexual freedom. Pornography and, by
association, Angelo, logically extend the socially accepted masculine role; by so doing they highlight the contradiction implicit in
the value which society and, earlier, Isabella assert to be a part of
the rational and virtuous use of authority: 'O, it is excellent/To have
a giant's strength, but it is tyrannous/To use it like a giant' (II, ii,
108–10) may be a plea for the gentle exercise of power and strength

but it is also a contradiction in terms. Whatever strength a giant uses must be a giant's strength – he can do no other. Similarly, Angelo's corruption is as inevitably a function of his masculinity as of his authority. His abuse of his judicial function is compounded by, as it stems from, the sexual relation between himself and the woman he tyrannizes. Angelo's discovery of his maleness, of his quintessential self, because it comes so late in his life is uncontrollable. He reveals a kind of anxiety about his use of power which seems to arise, as Coppélia Kahn puts it, 'from the disparity between men's social dominance and their peculiar emotional vulnerability to women'.[8] Angelo lacks the habit of male authority over women which is one of the defining features of the world of the play. That his discovery of his masculinity should be coincident with his acquisition of power is no accident. For each feeds the other. The pornographic act is contingent upon the possession of power; and to one untutored in the world's ways of sexuality – that is, the easy and casual exercise of male sexual authority – the temptations for exercise of sexual freedom are irresistable.

There is, of course, a kind of despair in Angelo's brutality. As his whole being is subdued by Isabella's presence, eyes, and voice, so he reaches in his helplessness for such weapons as life affords to overcome the new sensation. The weapons are the considerable ones of apparently absolute power; and in his anguish at what he is about to do and at what has become of him he employs this power as his blood dictates he must. The potential danger of the possession of great power is thus underlined because, as the play demonstrates, it is wielded by men of flesh and blood.

That Isabella should associate sexuality with pain and death and an agonizing death with flamboyant suffering is a natural and logical consequence of her present plight and her personal history. She chooses death over degradation as a means of retaining that spiritual purity which she sees debased by men. Angelo uses sex to destroy her and Claudio is prepared to use her sexuality to rescue himself. Looking around her from the perspective of one whose appeals to men for kindness and mercy are met with the sheerest sexual exploitation, it is no wonder that Isabella sees an 'injurious world' (IV, iii, 122) and little but 'corruption in this life' (III, i, 232). At every turn she is confronted by men who would steal her vocation from her. First seen expressing a wish to chart her own destiny in life, she is interrupted in her decision by Lucio. From there her affairs are a series of dreadful encounters with the male

world of power which she has tried to avoid or escape; from
Angelo's brutality she is thrust into the presence of Claudio who
attempts to move her by his weakness. The Friar who manipulates
her into helping Mariana turns out to be the Duke of Vienna himself
who also reveals, finally, a sexual interest in Isabella. His proposal
of marriage includes a reminder of Isabella's debt to him and is thus
not an opportunity for her to make a choice freely based upon her
natural inclination:

> If he be like your brother, for his sake
> Is he pardon'd; and for your lovely sake
> Give me your hand and say you will be mine.

> (V, i, 488–90)

'His sake' and 'your lovely sake' are nicely complementary, and
notwithstanding the gallantry of the latter, enforce attention to the
unstated dependency of each upon the other. The juxtaposition of
the rescue of Claudio and the proposal that Isabella marry the
rescuer is suspicious. There is arrogance in the Duke's assumption
of the connection between his authority and his sexuality. His
proposal indicates his belief that Isabella should acknowledge such
associations in her own mind. When the Duke asks Isabella to 'say
you will be mine' he is transcending the banality of the *cliché*. What
F. R. Leavis seems insufficiently to have considered in his vindi-
cation of the play and the Duke is the extent to which the Duke's
commitment to a conservative ideology has been undercut, subverted and challenged by the events and language of the drama. His
confident assertion that the Duke's 'attitude, nothing could be
plainer, *is* meant to be ours – his total attitude, which is the attitude
of the play'[9] – neglects the way in which the Duke's attitude is itself
an ideological form which has been questioned throughout, and
which inevitably triumphs because it is an expression of Vienna's
dominant power structure, not because it is an inherently 'right'
attitude. Vincentio is using his own authority to assert his male
supremacy and his male right to possess his woman. He does not
say, in response to her silence, that he will be hers, but, rather
differently, 'What's mine is yours, and what is yours is mine' (l.
534). Nowhere in the proposal is Isabella's wish consulted. Instead
it is merely assumed to be compliant with that of the higher power
of the Duke. It is hard, then, not to see in Isabella's response to the
Duke's marriage proposals the silence of despair and resignation.

'or in her encounters with the men in the play, Isabella is not called
ipon to act but, rather, to submit her will, her dignity, and her
lestiny.

Shunted from one crisis to the next from the moment she leaves
he convent, Isabella is brought face to face with that self she has
ought to deny by abjuring the company of men. Returned to
ociety she is buffeted by the men of Vienna whose actions serve
igain and again to remind her of her femaleness – her gender is
lefined for her by their attitudes. These are universally the atti-
udes that follow logically and inevitably from their perceptions of
ier and themselves in a sexual relationship that stems in each case
rom the social condition of the genders as they relate to one
inother. Thus her acceptance of guidance from the disguised Duke
– her spiritual adviser – and its cataclysmic outcome constitutes a
lramatic reversal of Isabella's initial attempt to forge a life for
ierself that is free of the forces of male influence. Having surren-
lered her will and, in some measure her moral sense, to 'Friar
_odowick' she is deceived and betrayed by him too. But his direc-
ion has a purpose very satisfactory for the male ethic of the society
>f Vienna. Through his agency Isabella, a powerful questing spirit
ull of the determination of heroic selfhood is reduced – some would
iay elevated – to womanliness. For the Isabella who pleads upon
>ended knee before Duke Vincentio to save the life of the
nurderous Angelo for the sake of Mariana's happiness is just the
<ind of female that the men in this drama esteem. Upon her knee
ihe most closely resembles the spirit of femininity cherished by
Vienna's men. Bowed, supplicating, softly virtuous, Isabella's
ethical climax is also her most palpable defeat:

> Most bounteous sir:
> Look, if it please you, on this man condemn'd
> As if my brother liv'd. I partly think
> A due sincerity govern'd his deeds
> Till he did look on me. Since it is so,
> Let him not die. My brother had but justice,
> In that he did the thing for which he died:
> For Angelo
> His act did not o'ertake his bad intent,
> And must be buried but as an intent
> That perish'd by the way. Thoughts are no subjects;
> Intents but merely thoughts.

(V, i, 442–52)

This plea and the restoration of Claudio do not suddenly efface the past. Isabella and Angelo make no peace with each other. These are her last words in the drama; for the rest she watches as a greater power than hers unfolds itself. She watches Angelo's passionate shame; she watches Claudio's return to society; and she watches Vincentio punish Lucio more cruelly than he punishes Angelo, Lucio her brother's one true friend; and she watches Vincentio exercise complete control over the lives of all of his subjects including herself as he proposes to pluck her from the path she has intended for her life. There is no way of ever knowing how Shakespeare intended this last scene. All we can be sure of is, in Harriet Hawkins's eloquent words, that he has deprived the characters 'of human and dramatic dignity by denying them the full measure of responsibility that comes from facing the consequences of their own decisions and desires'.[10] And it is in this that Angelo and Isabella are finally alike. Two powerful characters propelled to act and to know with a nearly measureless intensity are diminished to crass anonymity; they dwindle into a husband and a wife, and are made to stand by acutely aware of what is being done to them, but equally aware that they are helpless to do anything about it. Their powerful individuality, unleashed by the dark and incomprehensible force of sex, is merely domesticated in this concluding spectacle. Though both Isabella and Angelo have been profoundly altered by their knowledge of that force and of its existence deeply within themselves, their resocializing is a way of simplifying and, even, negating the changes that have occurred.

4   The Transforming
Audiences of *Richard II*

In his book on reading the novel, Wolfgang Iser alerts us to the activity of reading, to the way in which the reader is always an implied participant in the composition of the novel's meaning.[1] The reader's function, that is, is not merely to absorb the words of the fiction but, rather, to discover its meaning and thus perform as an organic part of its composition. The play audience is similarly a part of the process of completion, though is not always recognized as such. A commonly received notion of the reader and spectator of drama is that of a passive and distant observer of the narrative. Kristian Smidt, by way of example, depicts this passivity with the statement that, 'as readers or spectators, we are brought into an imagined setting and await developments'.[2] The idea of us waiting, in a sense obviously true, does not, however, sufficiently declare the process of reading or observing a play; it does not acknowledge the way in which the reader or spectator is changed by the experience or how he changes the text by that same experience. There is a wealth of literature on watching characters watching other characters in Shakespearean dramas but not a great deal on the way in which the act of watching is imitated by the audience – though the irony of this fact is always duly noted – and how that act in the audience transforms the action within the text. Critics have tended to concentrate upon those scenes in which watching takes the form of spying, in which, in other words, the character invites the audience or reader to observe him watching another character unnoticed by him. And yet, of course, the action of sequential dialogue always implies watching. As a character delivers himself of his lines he watches his addressee as he responds: this is no less true of stychomythic sequences than of the long speeches in the presence of one or many auditors.

The function of the audience or reader is a chief subject of the deposition scene in *Richard II*. Having smashed the mirror, Richard addresses Bolingbroke with the words, 'Mark, silent king' (IV, i,

290), thus adding to the title a curiously significant adjective which
has the effect of underscoring what may be called Bolingbroke's
method during the scene. That method has been to stand back and
watch as Richard, whom James Winny has called 'the ecstatic com-
mentator',[3] spends himself through the medium of his words,
knowing as he surely does, that the language Richard speaks is
self-enclosed, reflexive upon itself and, thus ultimately impotent in
any real political terms. Bolingbroke, then, the true source of political authority in this scene, has chosen silence as mode of control.
What Richard does or says here is done or said because Bolingbroke
permits it and for no other reason. The most dramatic and violent
act of the scene, the dashing of the mirror to the ground is accomplished for the reason, simply, that Bolingbroke orders, 'Go some of
you, and fetch a looking-glass' (IV, i, 267). By the order itself and
notwithstanding his otherwise silent observation of Richard,
Bolingbroke declares his authority. Part of that authority is shown,
as well, in his allowing Richard to play out his delusion, in permit-
ting Richard the illusion of control over his own version of the
events being enacted. The compact, with himself, of silent observation, and the decision to allow the play to go on is precisely the
compact made by the reader or spectator with himself and the form
with which he is engaged. The audience has the power to stop the
play – and as history tells us, has frequently availed itself of this
power – as Bolingbroke has here the power to stop the play, to
assert his mastery over the form which Richard has adopted.[4]

Richard's performance is observed by other characters than
Bolingbroke. Present as well as those lords who support the usurper
is a group of nobles who will try to stop his progress and who will
pay in different ways for their failure to so. They too silently
witness the deposition, affecting a neutrality they do not feel. This
is one of those occasions when, as Moody E. Prior remarks 'to
proclaim neutrality is in effect to take sides'.[5] By their silence they
side with Bolingbroke during the process, by their private later
declarations they negate that position. The dividedness of this
audience to the deposition is interestingly paralleled by the
dividedness of readers of the play who have been directed by
influential critics to taking sides with Richard or Bolingbroke,
though the trend at present seems to acknowledge a persistent
ambivalence within the drama and the playwright's refusal to
champion either at the expense of the other.[6]

The deposition scene is, I think, a special exception to John

Wilders' generally true statement that Shakespeare's kings reveal themselves 'more vividly in intimate private situations than in council chambers or in the market place'.[7] In part this exception is a consequence of Shakespeare having provided Richard with few private moments and only one soliloquy in the entire play. And yet, throughout the drama Richard shows a tendency towards soliloquy by virtue of what Joseph Porter calls his 'unmarked direction of address' which produces 'the subtle effect of his talking to himself even when he appears to be talking to others'. This tendency, Porter continues, 'manifests his tending towards solipsism and iso-lation'.[8] Richard's solopsism has often been commented on and is, at least by one critic, regarded as the chief reason for his disquali-fication as a tragic hero.[9] But it is that very quality which Shake-speare employs as the basis of his theatrical mimesis. Because Richard so self-consciously directs so much of his speech in this scene towards himself, his audiences are driven to watching him as though he were alone, as though the process of transformation being witnessed by them is occurring in private. The responses of his onstage audience, hostile or sympathetic, is mirrored in the criticism and probably reflects thoughtful audience reactions over the ages. These responses derive, of course, from the dramatic action of the scene, an action which is both, to use Leonard Barkan's description, 'the raveling and unraveling of a fictional narrative', and 'a sequence of emotional responses, both among the characters on stage and between stage characters and members of the audience'.[10] The onstage audience of this scene is more deliberately and vividly an audience than usual. This is no heath with a mad king and a watching fool. The scene is a theatrical occasion made more obviously so by virtue of the presence onstage of a large group of spectators: one of those climactic moments of the play described by Robert Ornstein as 'ceremonies of ascension and declension acted out on the heights and depths of the playhouse stage'.[11]

Notwithstanding the privacy of Richard's performance the soliloquy quality of his speeches in the scene makes the speeches work like internal monologues. However much the major moments of his addresses might be directed inwardly, however much they stand as self-justifications and self-accusations, their effect is felt on his audiences in the way that Shakespearean soliloquies are felt in the tragedies. The suffering man is seen here examining his anguish as though it were in some sense separate from himself, a rare and precious jewel being held up to the pitiless light of a public theatre. Despite the self-absorbed loneliness of the monarch, in other words, his words and directions are absolutely dependent upon the presence of that silent audience. This on one level is obvious, though it is perhaps less easy to know his motive with equal certainty. He has gone beyond – and he recognizes this – preserving himself from his enemy because, clearly, his enemy has gone beyond being able to halt the rush of his own movement towards power. But history furnishes us with a multitude of great orations by doomed men and women whose motives though various have in common a need to justify, explain, and, perhaps above all, to defy the authority that has defeated them while acknowledging its power. One thing is inarguable, however, about all such situations: that is that the motive on both sides, the motive to speak and the motive to permit speech, is the *fact* of the audience. But the audience has a function in such scenes as that played between Richard and Bolingbroke, a function which far transcends its presence as witness to the events. The audience, by being there, defines certain limits for the actors in the drama. That is, while the audience is being used by Bolingbroke on one level and Shakespeare on another level, having been allowed or invited, its presence declares the existence of an unstated but precisely delineated contract. That contract is an acknowledgement of the political implications of the theatrical form which, no less than the content or theme of the drama, is ideological.

In discussing the image of the play in Shakespearean drama Anne Righter has demonstrated that the image is a 'technique for maintaining contact with the spectators'.[12] That contact is all important. The spectator can be, as Paul Gaudet has convincingly argued with reference to the 'parasitical' counselors, reflectors of the speaker. Bushy Bagot and Greene are important 'as indicators or signifiers, as one of the means by which Shakespeare manipulates his audience's response to the main contending forces of the play'.[13] Their efficacy as reflectors lies very much in their silent passivity. The same may surely be said of the spectators of the deposition whose silent presence is more than merely scenic; it is offered as a kind of testing ground for the ideas and ideologies, individual and social, which are in such violent contention in the arena which Bolingbroke has formed. The theatre audience and the onstage audience to the deposition are finally ambiguous in this case in their responses to the manipulations of the playwright. They need to choose between the two kinds of values presented. Bolingbroke's strength is in his promise of social order – an attractive proposition to most – while Richard's strength is to present, dramatically, the human cost of that order. The two audiences need either to choose between them or, at least, to acknowledge their equal force.

The public deposition is a consequence of Bolingbroke's having made a choice to provide Richard with an audience. The choice is determined by a multiplicity of forces, among them the possibility that the forum will exonerate the usurper who will control the events of the deposition, it will demonstrate the necessity of usurpation in the extreme situation which seems to have come about because of the failure of Richard to maintain order in his realm. The limitation of Bolingbroke's control is Richard's freedom of speech which, as previous events seem to have shown, Bolingbroke has no great reason to fear. But the deposition scene is different. Here Richard already knows that he is vanquished, that he must die, that there is nothing left for him to lose. The scene thus becomes fraught not with a defeated sense of inevitability, but with surprise, with the unexpected. Richard here combines his knowledge of the nature of his audience with the knowledge of his impending death. The result is an almost sudden tilt in a new direction. There is a moment in the deposition scene when the king tears himself away from his anchor of self-pitying egotism. Evident at that instant is separation of himself from his emotional history in a manner that adumbrates and initiates a movement towards knowing in ways that are radically new for him. The whole play seems to shift on its axis with Richard's crucial departure from habit and tendency. The shift occurs because of the participation of Northumberland – one of the generally silent audience with which Richard has been surrounded. In departing from his role as spectator and adopting that of stage manager or director, Northumberland forces departures from the political or social texts which have been formed in advance. Neither he nor Bolingbroke, nor anyone else who watches the ceremony, can have accounted for the perverse and unpredictable nature of human nature. Richard has been asked for a second time by Northumberland to read the articles of his crimes against the nation in the ceremony of public confession. The king responds:

> Mine eyes are full of tears, I cannot see.
> And yet salt water blinds them not so much
> But they can see a sort of traitors here.

> Nay, if I turn mine eyes upon myself,
> I find myself a traitor with the rest.

> (IV, i, 244–8)

It is this blurring of his vision, this involuntary assertion of the physical self over the psychological which cannot be anticipated. It causes Richard to confuse external and internal worlds. Around him through his tears he sees his audience, and through his tears that audience is one homogeneous gathering of traitors. Looking within he discovers himself to be merely another of the sinister throng. This act of self-critical introspection, utterly contingent upon the presence of his audience, is a kind of obedience to the laws of physiology and poetry. Richard cannot, of course, literally turn his eyes upon himself and see anything clearly, and yet of course, the blurred vision forces him to blink, to seem to look inward. But the declaration that he is looking inward introduces a new note of consciousness to the entire drama and compels him to look elsewhere than at his reflecting audience for a reminder of who he is. The statement, that is, that he is looking inside himself is almost as important for his self-discovery as the act of doing it. Looking at his audiences has always been Richard's way of defining himself – whether at his friends or his enemies. The faces of his friends and enemies have always told him who he is. But here he is forced to look inside himself and sees himself as another reflector. The dramatic power of the passage lies with the line, 'Nay, if I turn mine eyes upon myself', and within that line upon the word 'if'. The word possesses both conditional and temporal connotations as Richard uses it, and both meanings ring with simultaneous truth. The uncertainty which the word contains helps represent a Richard poised dangerously on the brink of new discoveries. Its temporal implication serves as a reminder that the experience of turning inward is new for Richard, and its consequences, so long looked for and so egregiously lacking until now, must be to lead him away from that former self to a different and, perhaps, profounder awareness. The act however, because introspective, has the additional and surprising effect of separating Richard from his audience further than has been the case. For by introducing his private self to that audience he is alluding to a world of experience which they cannot know; he is placing a

mystery at their feet and yet continuing to assert its mysterious-
ness.

Having declared himself to be one with his audience, Richard
becomes capable of seeing himself reflected within himself: he
becomes, for the first time in the play, part of that reflecting image
of the kind which has been the function of the external world until
this point. As the process of self-discovery hinges upon the perception of an inner audience, the climax of the discovery is the
breaking of the mirror. But this act, in turn, develops naturally from
the insight, for it demonstrates the inadequacy of the kind of
self-apprehension upon which the king has relied until this
moment – that vain sort of knowledge whereby the self is known
entirely as a compound of his audience's reflection of it. The mirror,
Prior reminds us, 'carries complex iconographic and literary
echoes. It was used as a symbol of vanity and pride and at the same
time as an image of truth'.[14] But Richard dashes it to the ground
because it reflects only a partial truth; it reflects what his audiences
have always shown at a moment when he has come to know the
inadequacy of the external world as a reflector of truth. His audiences have, in a sense, created the self that Richard has known till
now. The 'flatt'ring glass' reflects only his face. By breaking it
Richard shows his awareness of the momentousness of his new
knowledge. Though Barkan is justified in reading the play as a
'history of violent or passionate energies, suppressed and then
released',[15] the shattering of the glass is the first act of real violence
in a drama that has promised many such. Its motive lies in the act of
looking inwards, an act which leads to the discovery of the great
discrepancy between the two worlds of his existence – the one
ephemeral and dependent upon the way in which he is seen by his
persistent audience, the other newly discovered world, constant
and authentically felt. The first part of the drama can in this sense be
seen as an almost compulsive avoidance of the self by seeking its
reality in the eyes, acts, and faces of those who look upon him,
while, with the crucial discovery, the remainder constitutes a
coming to terms with that individual part of his audience, himself,
alone capable of bringing to light those sides of the self which have
been forced into the shadows by the reflections surrounding it.
Thus here are thought and act drawn into a marvellous harmony,
with the one leading for the first time in the play, by the ineffable
force of dramatic logic, into the other. What Tillyard has noted of
the play as a whole, that its actions 'tend to be symbolic rather than

real',[16] is certainly true of the play until this point at least.

The violence of the action vividly draws Richard's audiences, it disrupts and dislocates the flow of events; breaking the glass is an act of utter finality, replacing the noise of voices with a new strange sound of destruction. The mirror contains a part of Richard's former self, 'crack'd in an hundred shivers' (IV, i, 289). It has been destroyed, as he says, by his sorrow, a symptom of his suffering. Sorrow has brought his tears and sorrow has impelled his violence. Through sorrow Richard is thrust onto the uncharted paths of study of that inner audience which had been all but stifled by the other audience to his life. The effect of suffering upon the mind of Richard is to make him question the entirety of that past life which has been concentrated in the reflection in the glass and in the faces of his subjects. His acknowledgement of his own complicity with his audience of traitors is a recognition of his own role as an audience to himself and simultaneously the inadequacy of that role and the consequent need to annihilate that self.

The violence and the nihilistic language which accompanies it is perhaps the most shocking of Richard's departures from the role which Bolingbroke has created for him. Rather than passively doing what is expected of him, the act 'wrenches attention inwards to Richard, the more designedly in that it seems to complete a movement apparent through the whole score'.[17] 'I have no name, no title' (IV, i, 255) refers to more than the mere fact that he has lost his formal role; it raises the fear that he has lost his past. Richard seems to recognize that his identity has been stolen from him because, in part, that former self has been so detachable or external by virtue of its capacity wholly to be defined by others or himself as a kind of other or audience to his royalty. Rossiter's observation about Richard's *'lack of inside'*[18] in the early scenes seems to me to conform to part of a deliberate poetic design which underscores this incapacity to know himself except as an observed phenomenon, as a creature on a stage. The early Richard is a series of voices and postures, all conforming to stereotypical notions of a stage king. There, in those scenes preceding the great perception initiated by his tears in the deposition scene, Richard's appearances are theatrical occasions for display of a self which conforms both physically and passionally to the image of a king. Even there the spontaneous language is precisely connected to the theatrical posture, as Joseph Porter has well noted about such apparently sudden passionate language when, for example, Richard interrupts

Gaunt's warning with his 'lunatic lean-witted fool' speech, where Richard 'is thinking absolutely of his "external manners" – thinking of himself merely as perceived by others'.[19] Time and again in his melancholy moments he alludes to what we might call idealized sensations which find their inspiration in images from the world external to himself. It is not, for example, the kingliness which the 'water from the rough rude sea' (III, i, 54) cannot wash from Richard but the balm (the make-up) by which he was annointed. His focus remains impersonal: 'Have I not reason to *look* pale and dead?' (III, ii, 79; my italics). 'Is not the king's *name* twenty thousand names?' (III, ii, 85; my italics). Even the portrait of the angel of death keeping court 'within the hollow crown/That rounds the mortal temples of a king' (III, ii, 160–1) evades the actually threatened kingship of Richard himself. His depiction of himself in monk-like poverty is a further idealization of the exchange of one role – the gorgeous royal self – for another in merely opposite terms, with both roles presented for the entertainment of an audience, both deriving theatrical efficacy from the accoutrements of the roles which he presents as defining the man.

Richard is a poet to the extent that his speeches are always forms of communication whose meaning is dependent upon their apprehension and acknowledgement by his audience. His language in the 'exchange' speech is designed around a set of commonplace signs to be replaced by another such set. The transmogrification of the monarch, defined by the signifiers of monarchy, is completed by the replacement of an opposite system of signifiers. He merely switches roles for his audience, appealing to them in terms of immediately comprehensible iconographic traditions. All is, in Richard's mind, easily and suddenly accomplished by the mere fact of saying so. But in life and in good art – Shakespeare's not Richard's – knowledge and change are harder won than the king here knows and as he must painfully learn. Life's important and altering decisions are never free and unencumbered as he seems to feel in this speech; they are never the pure exercise of free will; such are the mere fantasies of tepid poets like the Richard who would change his gay apparel for an almsman's gown. Reality has a habit of jarring such lyrical self-indulgence in the form of other people and larger power than one's own, and enforcing new and unforeseen motives upon one. In the deposition scene, Richard's audience has changed its composition and thus redefined the terms of his expression. The context of his world is reshaped by the

circumstances of Bolingbroke's ascent to the throne. And it is in the
new context, before a newly constituted audience that Richard, no
longer free to indulge mere fantasies and ideologies, seeks and
finds motives within a self that has not before seen the light.

In the halls of Westminster, surrounded by men who would
depose and kill him, by an audience of enemies onstage and a
theatre audience of undetermined composition, the paean to
poverty and the hermit's life seems no more than an idle dream. It is
surely the composition of the audience that encourage Richard to
discover new resources within himself. His suffering is not
measurably made greater by the new circumstances, but his
audience, having declared itself, is a kind of inspiration to inward-
ness. The inspiration derives in part from an acceptance at last of
his own powerlessness to change the political situation as is testi-
fied by the audiences to whom he must now represent himself.
Bolingbroke's power derives from his skill in integrating the past
with the present, in building upon what has happened in order to
shape the present, made dramatically manifest in the deposition
scene with Richard's entry. Richard's previous view of Bolingbroke
included the sight of Bolingbroke kneeling before him. But now, in
Westminster, the act of submission is recognized to have been
ironic at best, cruelly sarcastic at worst. For now Richard enters in
clear submission to the will of the usurper.

> Alack, why am I sent for to a king
> Before I have shook off the regal thoughts
> Wherewith I reign'd?

> (IV, i, 162–4).

The question reflects more than the uncertainty it implies. It contains a luminous awareness of the ambiguity of experience. The
material elements of the present scene enforce upon Richard an
awareness of the contradictions of his immediate experience and
then, as his physical senses become affected by his plight, all of his
life.

The presence of spectators to his deposition is a powerful means
through which Richard constructs his identity. The strength of his
language comes from his recognition of their presence and the
presence of irony which the fact of being observed by his erstwhile
subjects implies. This, then, the centrally illuminating scene of the

play, abounds in a kind of doubleness as the stage is suddenly
crowded with, essentially, two monarchs of one kingdom; with a
descending king whose energy and defiance come from the sight of
his opposite mounting ever higher, and whose speech resounds
with hard-won irony as it reacts to the self-contradictory image. The
'blunt realism of Bolingbroke',[20] who vainly tries to direct Richard's
attention to the matter at hand in such prosaic, but pointed remarks
as, 'I thought you had been willing to resign', (IV, i, 914) and 'Are
you contented to resign the crown?' (IV, i, 200) provides Richard's
searching mind with the evidence of an audience and the impetus
for public analysis of his condition. In each of Bolingbroke's
remarks Richard finds a sign by following which he is able to
identify an additional element in his condition. And yet, while the
knowledge that he is the victim of his acknowledged audience
seems initially to provide him with a certain pleasure and an occasion for martyrish display, the discovery through the process of the
rhetoric of his own complicity in his downfall seems to alter the
direction of his performance. Initially he is capable of objectifying
his experience very largely through the mediation of imagery by
which the crown becomes an external property, capable of containing symbolically the process of suffering. The world he inhabits in
this early part of the deposition scene is capable of reduction to a
history of the monarchy and an iconographic representation of the
politics of state religion. The significance of these 'signs' is in their
existence as points of contact – of similarity – between the actor and
his audience and thus, also, as points of difference and departure
from them. Richard's self-deposition, notoriously recognized by
Walter Pater as an inversion of the coronation ritual[21] is curiously
impersonal, especially in the shrill intensity of the last lines of the
speech:

> Long may'st thou live in Richard's seat to sit,
> And soon lie Richard in an earthy pit.
> God save King Henry, unking'd Richard says,
> And send him many years of sunshine days!
> What more remains?

> (IV, i, 218–22)

The insincerity of the benediction by which Richard, with a crushing sarcasm crowns Henry, is capped by the tragic, devastating

businesslike question at the end of the speech. John Baxter has
indeed, pointed out that Richard 'seems to resort to the plain style
in moments of resignation hovering on the edge of despair'.[22]

This scene with its insistent use of concrete objects and its physical emphases removes the king from his world of abstraction and
plunges him with a nearly palpable force into the world of the
physical and the tactile, that world which, in this drama of expected
violence, is a major point of connection with both his audiences – an
additional means of drawing in those audiences by common experience. Richard enters and removes his crown which is then used
in a vivid tug-of-war with Bolingbroke as the two antagonists come
as physically close to touching each other as any action in the play is
capable of suggesting. Then he lays aside the concrete signifiers of
his monarchy, his crown and sceptre. Thereafter Northumberland
provides him with yet another prop, a paper containing a list of
accusations and crimes. Following this accumulation of tangible
properties, comes the acknowledgement from Richard that his
mind is so affected by the events of the moment that his physical
being has responded by blinding him with tears. This 'blinding' is
the immediate precursor to the bringing of the mirror which is
flung upon the ground and broken. At the centre of this process by
which the momentum of events is augmented through increasing
the number of objects onstage, is the physical reaction of the protagonist. For as the objects are external to his person, supplied from
elsewhere, the tears are his own, and it is in response to his tears
that Richard is most affected. The discovery of the paradox of his
complicity with his betrayers makes Richard a spectator of his own
deposition and cements the connection of himself to his world, a
connection which he denied until his weeping helped him see it.

Tears, as Scott McMillin has perceptively shown, are agents of the
truth in *Richard II*; though those who observe others weeping are
incapable of perceiving the clarifying function of tears.[23] Northumberland is one such whose externality to the weeping Richard is
stressed by his emotional distance from moral shocks which
Richard is undergoing. As Richard concludes a thought, Northumberland, an active spectator to the events, tries to return him to the
business of reading the articles, urging Richard to attend less to
himself and more to the business at hand. Shakespeare underscores
a moral difference between Bolingbroke and Northumberland, and
thus heightens the ambiguity of the possible responses to the two
contenders, by giving to Bolingbroke words of compassion and

one to Northumberland. For even Bolingbroke, who has the most to gain by the king's attention to the articles, summons the compassion to put a stop to the pressing requests – 'Urge it no more, my lord Northumberland' (IV, i, 271). But, of course, Northumberland's insistence is essential to the process of illumination: he directs Richard towards a new way of seeing himself and thus the audiences of the deposition towards a new way of seeing Richard. Northumberland is an active mediator here between the drama of self-discovery and the drama of observing that process. By urging Richard yet again, 'My lord, dispatch, read o'er these articles' (IV, i, 243), he sets in motion the crucial progress of sequential logic by which the king finally turns his eyes upon himself simultaneously with the discovery that he cannot see to read. All attention is concentrated upon the related images and accompanying act of seeing and reading, of reading the papers and reading the self in a remarkably similar way. Sight here is compounded by some of the facets of the verb *to see* – to see is to read, to read is to know, to know is to be aware both of the physically real – the contents of the papers – and the immaterially real – the urgently tormenting self as it almost instinctually asserts its reality in the contexts in which the self operates. Thus the papers containing a partial reflection of the self are brought into a fascinating conjunction with that more complex inner self through the agency of the image. 'Mine eyes are full of tears, I cannot see', thus becomes profoundly and, because of its implications of suffering, movingly ironic as the idea and the image of sight coalesce in the powerful intimation of higher sight, of wisdom about the locus of the self in a reordered universe whose reordering has been determined with the demands of the audiences foremost. Richard knows with a disturbing certainty that he is himself guilty:

> Nor no man's lord. I have no name no titles;
> No, not that name was given me at the font.

> (IV, i, 252–6)

Though he relapses into the mode of self pity, the anger has come. While it is soon quenched, for the moment of its existence the entire play is transformed by it and leads Richard in new directions. For, as his audiences are typically lulled by the sheer sadness of the hero – as Bolingbroke's expression of pity actively demonstrates –

tempted by the growing pathos and inevitablity of the conclusion
the flash of anger is a sudden astringent to despair, causing the king
momentarily to tense his muscle, to react hostilely rather than
succumb. In a sense, Richard's anger is an expression of optimism
For, while it no way suggests that he will be able to surmount his
lot, it shows a desire for confrontation. In the single line, 'No lord o
thine thou haught insulting man', and by his own energy and
passion, Richard brings himself to face his audience, represented
here in its antipathetic self by Northumberland; and he raise
himself from a position of surrender to one of superiority. By hi
rage he reduces that audience as he elevates himself. In that ele
vation, in the switching of his emotional levels merely by the
spontaneous discovery of a residue of wrath, he gains an unpre
dictable command over those who are watching him.

Though much of what follows in the scene is a reversion to th
'half-rhetorical, half lyrical'[24] style, again Richard unexpectedl
flashes with an emotion which stands in contrast to the weltering
self-pity. He asks Bolingbroke,

> For I have given here my soul's consent
> T'undeck the pompous body of a king;
> Made glory base, and sovereignty a slave;
> Proud majesty a subject, state a peasant.

(IV, i, 249–52)

He refuses to take refuge in his words or to subsume his reason in
images of self-pity. By the strong and untypically succinct anti
theses of these lines Richard is made suddenly to seem emotionall
alive for, with the recognition of his own responsibility for hi
present condition, he has struck at an intellectually dynamic trut
which endues him with the new personal strength. Northumber
land's interruption, 'My lord –' (IV, i, 253) provides Richard wit
the occasion for some sharp fury which proceeds from the discover
of inner strength: 'No lord of thine, thou haught insulting man' (IV
i, 254).

The scene becomes electrified by a sudden tilt in emotional ton
through which the character of the king is given crucial depth
Anger, strength and pride are captured in this outburst of invectiv
which, by the dynamic contrast it makes to the mood of the pre
ceding lines, lends some intimation of the heroic capacity whic

ιdversity can bring. The flash of rage indicates a refusal to submit to
he oppressive design etched for him by his enemies – his watching
ιudience – and a capacity for resistance to tyranny. For the seconds
he line takes to be uttered, Richard shows a measure of 'inside'
which, however, dissipates in the very next utterance:

> Rich.   . . . Proud majesty a subject, state a peasant.
> North.   My lord –
> Rich.   No lord of thine, though haught insulting man;
>   I'll beg one boon,
>   And then be gone, and trouble you no more.
>   Shall I obtain it?
> Bol.   Name it fair cousin.
> Rich.   Fair cousin! I am greater than a king;
>   For when I was king, my flatterers
>   Were then but subjects; being now a subject,
>   I have a king here to my flatterer.
>   Being so great, I have no need to beg.

> (IV, i, 302–9)

Bolingbroke's response provides this terrible and moving scene
with one of its most powerful moments. Shakespeare here brilliantly creates an occasion that is both fascinating and cryptic. For,
not only does the phrase 'fair cousin' provide the newly aware
Richard with the opportunity for a crushingly effective sarcasm,
but additionally it resonates with self-reflexive ambiguity. Bolingbroke's use of the phrase is heavy with disturbing implications. His
choice of this moment to allude to the blood tie that exists between
himself and Richard suggests, on the one hand, the disturbance of
his own heart, adumbrated by his earlier urging of Northumberland to desist; on the other hand it serves his interest to remind his –
not now Richard's – audience of his actual closeness to the throne.
His phrase, in short, speaks to both sides of the audiences of the
scene. In the act of separating himself from Richard, in parting from
him forever, he is contradictorily affirming the close connection
between them. The audiences are here forced into a recognition of
the essential ambivalence of the contending social and individual
values around which this scene of the drama is structured.

Richard's outburst, like that in which he refers to the loss of sight
through tears, is similarly structured around the idea of alternating

roles and divided audiences. He shows his growing awareness o
the purely functional nature of the personae of social living and o
their fragility. Being no longer king he is something else, just a:
being king he is something else. Such illuminations, superficia
though they may seem in their concentration upon the externals o
personality, are crucial to the illuminations about the internal sel
which are to come later. In Richard's bitter acknowledgement tha
he has a new role and that, as a consequence, his relations to hi:
world have been entirely reconstituted, he is forced to a recognitior
of the frailty of his former faith in his former persona. The speech
then, revolves around the issues of definition and redefinition, anc
the sarcasm of its tone provides a cutting edge by which Richar
lays bare the new situation. It is a situation which repeats the
discoveries of the preceding line but which, with one phrase, he
negates as he departs the chamber. He is all too quick to accep
Bolingbroke as the new king, thus acknowledging – as the silence o
that part of the onstage audience in conspiracy against Bolingbrok
acknowledges – the predominance of the world of actuality anc
power over the world of illusion and individual obsession in whicl
he dwelt. But, as he departs the chamber, Richard asserts the play':
eternal and recurrent truism in a couplet that almost simultaneousl}
negates it:

> O, good! Convey! Conveyers are you all
> That rise thus nimbly by a true king's fall.

> (IV, ii, 317–18)

The characteristically extravagant doubling of the couplet with the
second line's confident self image refers in all of its tersenes to the
ambivalent operation of the audience. On one level Richarc
conveys the abiding and inerasable sense of the play as a whole that
Bolingbroke's action is inherently futile and that Richard is King
Richard for all eternity. On another, subsequent events demonstrate the partial falsity of Richard's generalization – not *all* presen
are against him. The couplet as a whole, fulfilling what Baxter ha:
described as its function of 'holding the promise of moral and
political stability',[25] alludes to another sense which has intruded
upon the king's consciousness; that is, in its juxtaposition of the
two languages of the scene – that of the large imagination and tha
of realism – it reflects a lucid awareness of circumstance. As M. M.

Mahood has pointed out about this moment in the play, 'both king
and usurper now know there is no way of crossing the gulf between
the world of words and the world of things. The knowledge has
won the throne for Bolingbroke. It has also gained for Richard a
kingly dignity he did not possess as king'.[26]

Shortly before his exit, Richard described Bolingbroke as a
flatterer and continued his assault by describing those around him
as thieves – 'Conveyers are you all'. The line is reminiscent of a
more powerful line from *King Lear* when Lear with Cordelia dead
looks about him and cries at his audience, 'A plague upon you,
murderers traitors all!' (V, iii, 269). The assumptions of these two
lines from different plays are similar. Lear's line is more spectacularly and wildly wrong, being addressed, after all, to an
audience that includes such a character as Kent, who is as far from
being a murderer or a traitor as it is possible to get. The speaker
declares the hostile homogeneity of his audience onstage, that
audience which the text empowers him to acknowledge. The other
audience, the theatre audience, must respond to the declaration
with a mixture of sympathy for his plight and an awareness of the
error of his judgement. It is the response of those audiences which
drives the speaker back into himself. The audience onstage, by
watching the speaker and hearing his abuse, responds with silence.
The loudest voice the speaker hears is his own, and it forces him
both to cry more loudly and, simultaneously frustrated by his
searching, challenging invective, to return to himself as the stage's
sole source of knowledge and feeling.

Richard's choice of the word 'conveyers' to describe his audience
is an intriguing indicator of his coming to terms with a new reality
as signified by an increasingly mundane framework of invective
which becomes apparent within this scene. It is ironic that as
Richard's language becomes more earthbound, less grandiose and
less self-glorifying, he is brought to the recognition that his
moment of death is nearer. As he is driven relentlessly to the
periphery of the state of this world whose centre becomes solidly
occupied by Henry Bolingbroke, his speech begins to reflect a
belated knowledge of the sheer physical and political realities
which have thrust him aside. Looking around him as he first enters
Westminster, he sees himself surrounded by 'Pilates' and 'traitors'.
The designation of the usurpers in these terms is appropriate to his
own perceptions of himself as the divinely appointed deputy, the
true king of his nation. But gradually in the scene, with the esta-

blishment of a new more individual and personal conception of the situation, with the development of the knowledge that though he is no longer king, he is still alive, his invective takes on a dimension of toughness and realism which assists him to define himself anew and which challenges profoundly the moral intellect of his audiences. The audiences are compelled to react to his self-objectifications because, as linguistic objects they belong as much to those audiences as to the speaker. That is, if his enemies are Pilates, he is Jesus Christ. If his enemies are traitors then he is at very least a social being, at best a monarch. But, if his enemies are flatterers and thieves, he is simply a victim – one who has been robbed. Where earlier critics were prepared to take the comparison of himself to Christ as part of the play's Christian design, more recent critics have tended to be skeptical. James L. Calderwood, for example, argues that Richard's likening himself to Christ, 'instead of dignifying him as he surely intends it to do, . . . forces him to suffer an impossible comparison',[27] and Smidt suggests that the associations of himself with Christ, 'whether they are felt to be blasphemous or not are a sign of self-aggrandisement which, with its complement in self-abasement is a major fault of character'.[28]

While his terms of comparison and abuse of his audience are precise delineations of his apprehensions of those he hates, so are they indirectly, but no less precisely, modes of self-appraisal. The movement towards self-knowledge, given such eloquent voice throughout this scene, finds a blunt, but climactic expression in this moment of departure. And, indeed, it is in the couplet he speaks as he leaves the stage that Richard's perceptions are clearest. Here image and conviction coincide to produce the paradox for which Richard's deposition stands as an epitome and to which the division of his watchers testifies. For although, as Anne Righter has said, 'Richard the man and Richard the king have been separated',[29] Richard himself is strengthened by the knowledge that a man cannot be robbed of his past. That he has fallen in no way shakes his conviction which arises from the truly lived experience of his entire life, that whatever his title, he is the true king. Though he possesses the new capacity to see himself as a man, Richard's new knowledge refuses to negate and cannot erase or alter the old. The political reality of kingship provides Richard with an external context for his self-definition, but it becomes in the violent process of self-discovery a cypher of that external reality to which the inner self becomes linked. That Richard can still define himself as king is

ignificant not merely because the knowledge cements his belief in
his divine right to do so, but because it signifies his inevitable
connection to the world. The idea of kingship which has always
placed Richard in his world, now acquires additional force: the
word 'king' provides him with the objectively real fact to which he
can attach his whole being. His individual history is integrally
bound up with the connotations of the word and he glories in the
certainty that nothing can separate him from that perception of his
identity.

Richard's perceptions in this scene flow directly from the
presence of his audience whose function of watching is an essential
determinant of the ambiguity with which the theatre audience and
reader may respond to the process. The ambiguity is heightened by
an ubiquitous duality within the scene, a duality whose presence is
constant during the occupation of the stage by the two opposing
monarchs; it reaches a kind of emblematic climax during the
moment in which each of them clasps the crown. The language
Richard uses throughout the scene plays upon the idea of duality in
the many forms which it occupies during the course of the play. The
contrast of the figures onstage reinforces, by the styles to which
they are related, the same notion of a division in the world of
drama, a division which is made the more perceptible by the
analogical mode through which the theatre audience, in Marjorie
Garber's words, 'both compares and contrasts itself with the
audience constituted upon the stage'.[30] Northumberland and
Bolingbroke, blunt and brutal in turn, are another half of the coin of
which Richard forms the counterface. Though the audience is compelled by the persistent dualities of the scene to remain aware of the
play's ambiguities, Richard himself escapes the trap of ambiguity
through the painful process of self-discovery. For him, but not for
the audiences, the material and imaginative elements of the drama –
the tears and the pity – merge in a compelling perception by
Richard of his inner life in unrecognized forms. With this perception the tragic present acquires formal and logical structure. The *act*
of self-knowledge and its accompanying assertion give the individual an anchor in his world; they attach him more firmly to the
structure from which, in his ignorance, he threatens to depart. His
perception of himself as a traitor with the rest – obtained at a cost
that only he can know and that those watching him can only guess –
lends to Richard a new strength which derives from the dignity that
is the axiomatic concomitant of self-awareness.

5 The Alternating Narratives of *Twelfth Night*

All readers of Shakespeare are aware in differing degrees and ways of the ambiguity of the dramas: the tendency of Shakespearean criticism has been to create from inferences or cryptic structures within the plays an awareness of implicit alternative meanings in a work. For example, Ralph Berry and Norman Rabkin have demonstrated or persuasively suggested the existence of meanings of *Henry V* that drastically subvert the commonly held notions about the play. In Berry's words, 'Shakespeare's strategy is to keep his Crispin Crispian audience happy, while leaving on record the reservations that the "other" audience can pick up.'[1] And to Rabkin 'in *Henry V* Shakespeare created a work whose ultimate power is precisely the fact that it points in two opposite directions, virtually daring us to choose one of the two opposed interpretations it requires of us'.[2] The concern of these and most critics who are intrigued by the multivalence of Shakespearean drama remains, nonetheless, a concern with how Shakespeare meant, in a sense, to be misunderstood. Rabkin suggests that the more acute members of Shakespeare's early audiences might well have consisted of those who returned home from the theatre at least uncertain as to the meaning of what they had seen[3] (Berry's 'other' audience).

Much of the discussion about the meanings of the plays comes as a result of Shakespeare having made choices about the actions and behaviour of major characters which stood in simple defiance of some of the narrative laws by which the plays seem to have been written. Iago's refusal at the end to explain himself, or Isabella's silence in the face of Vincentio's marriage proposals, for example, overturn conventions of articulation upon which drama and its characters are based, and add considerable enigmas to the puzzle of the plays. And yet readers have to contend with the facts of Shakespeare's choices and, somewhat like characters in plays, find ourselves trying to understand and explain the presence of these choices as best we can. We might consider, for example, what critical emotions have been aroused in vituperation and exoneration of Prince Hal because Shakespeare chose, to almost no one's satis-faction (Samuel Johnson being a notable exception[4]) to have him stand forth alone onstage five minutes after he first appears and crave audience indulgence for his unacceptable behaviour. Such decisions about what happens in the story vitally affect the inter-pretations to which it must be subject. Of course it is true, in a sense, that every phrase uttered, every sound heard, every gesture performed 'happens in the story', and that these cumulatively determine the interpretation of its meaning. However, it is also traditional and usual to single out, as in the case of narrative, certain essential specific actions, decisions, and choices by the characters themselves as providing the impetus for the develop-ment of the events which lead the play to its conclusion. These moments are precisely different from those when, according to Ifor Evans, the narrative is suspended for the sake of style,[5] or precisely exemplified by those which Fredson Bowers has identified as the moments of the climax of the play.[6] Indeed, the example of Prince Hal's direct address to the audience does not, in fact, determine a future action, it is not the cause of an immediately following or future event in the play: it simply stands as an explanation of his behaviour. Certainly the presence of that address invites us to consider the effect and meaning of the same play without it; and doing so we come to realize just how fundamental a speech it really is. Though nothing else might change in its absence, the speech can be seen as the linchpin of the remainder of the entire cycle. Of course, it is easier to imagine a thing not done in a play than a thing done differently. Who would be so presumptuous as to write a speech for Isabella responding to Vincentio's proposal or for Iago telling all? And yet these alternative actions invite consideration just as our noting their absence points directly at their possible existence or presence?[7]

It is as obvious as it is true that each narrative implies an alter-native or hypothetical narrative which provides the basis for much of the criticism which the work generates. Sometimes Shakespeare is more obvious in pointing to the alternative hypothetical struc-ture of his drama than he is at others. *Hamlet* is a case in point. The constant vacillations of the prince revolve precisely around the dilemma of alternative actions. To act in one of two ways is Hamlet's choice. Whether to kill the king now or later, for example, is a question that allows him and us to see the problem of the alternative modes of action simultaneously. That is, the narrative of that drama incorporates both the actual story and the hypothetical story at once. Indeed, Hamlet's dilemma is the continuous possibility of two plays or two plots. Even, however, in the case of such works which are not so obviously about doubt and the conflicting magnetisms of two possible ways of behaviour, the alternative narration is implied. For as an action is taken, or a decision made, the possibility of an opposite or different action or decision is implied just as it is cancelled out. Some actions or episodes, however, occur not as result of the apparent choice of the character but because the playwright wills them to occur independently of the characters of the drama.

The first two scenes of *Twelfth Night* provide contrasting examples of the different effects and kinds of narrative modes within the drama and the concomitant dependence of the narrative upon certain kinds of behaviour. For in these two scenes are the alternating movements, moods, and characters of the plays put into opposing perspectives. The play shifts from passive to active life, from a static and effete world to one of dynamic vigour. Only at the end, with the undesigning contribution of Malvolio and the farcical subplot do the two worlds fuse in a mutually supportive harmony whereby the ideas and examples of indolence are banished together with those of disguise and panting, unrequited love. The 'normalcy' of the beginning of the play where the world mirrors an all too real confusion of idleness, loss, heartbreak, and envy, gives way to a dream world of realized hopes and fulfilled wishes.[8]

In the first scene nothing happens in the specialized sense that no word is uttered and no decision taken which in any way ruffle the placid surface of the scene. The calm spectacle of a lover languishing richly in his palace implies a comfortably enjoyed passion. Indeed, the language of the first speech climaxes again and again on notes of inaction, of reversion to images of stillness as in 'surfeiting', 'sicken, and so die', 'dying fall', 'sweet sound/That breathes' (I, i, 1–15). And notwithstanding the fact that the speech argues a restlessness of spirit, it doesn't suggest, promote, or invite an active response. It is no incentive to movement, but rather, an incentive to more of the same, more speechifying, more depiction of self. Four of Orsino's sentences in this brief first scene begin with the rhetorical, 'O', which in each case seems to signal the expression of an idea about to be addressed to the empty air or to himself rather than to any of the followers by whom he seems so lavishly to be urrounded. And his last words in the scene only reinforce the mage of indolent autointoxication so palpable in the words and novements of the spectacle:

> Away before me to sweet beds of flowers!
> Love-thoughts lie rich when canopied with bowers.

$$(I, i, 40-1)$$

On the other hand, with the second scene the play begins to move ahead with impressive rapidity, and the memory of Orsino fades nto inconsequence as Viola is seen to occupy the centre of the stage n her quick-fire and urgent questions as she, all too unsure of herself, dislocated and lost, needs to resolve those matters of life, ivelihood, and mere living taken for granted by the languid duke. Consider the events of the scene. Viola enters as herself; she leaves he stage some sixty-four lines later determined to become someone else. As T. W. Craik remarks, 'What is certainly suggested is that the apparent deadlock of the first scene is presently to be broken.'[9] Major events have occurred, actions have been taken, decisions made, each of which admits of an alternative. What we witness is a character obeying some deeper imperatives of her nature and simultaneously we can infer an author determining these imperatives in advance. Viola begins by rapidly taking stock of her situation after having survived a shipwreck in which she believes her brother may have been drowned – where am I? she asks, how shall I live? who governs here? whom does he love? The answer to each of the questions helps her to form a plan. When her first plan to serve the lady beloved of the duke is shown by the captain to be impracticable, she immediately changes her intention and determines instead to serve the duke who loves the lady. We can discern in this scene a very powerful narrative line, one that is based upon a series of far-reaching decisions, and one which, while reflective of character, almost subsumes everything else to *its* purpose and direction. This scene is about getting the drama begun. Yet it represents in many ways a number of crucial artistic decisions which determine, not always easily or clearly, the intention of the work. For example, why does this scene follow that depicting Orsino at home rather than precede it? Why does Shakespeare choose, in other words, to present Orsino in his comfortable palace as a background to Viola's crisis rather than the other way around?

While the actual answer to such questions cannot be known with any certainty, we can at least argue for the artistic sense of the arrangement of these two alternative scenes. It can be noted that the play's first scene provides a requisite background, in its colour and tone, for the violent and melancholy love stories which it seems to emcompass. It is a spacious and too-vivid spectacle of florid feelings being displayed. The conclusion, being in a manner, implied by the beginning, is thus contained within the extensive limits of that beginning. Orsino's court, its very air of indolence, notwithstanding the cloying extravagance with which it is charged, is larger than the rest of the play's actions, anticipates them and thus diminishes them. The lip service Orsino pays to love's pain and suffering, though commonplace, is sufficient to absorb and contain them when they are actually seen to occur. Thus, when in the second scene Viola appears and is observed to seize with vigorous determination such opportunities as occur, she is doing so against the background of an audience memory of the opening spectacle. The sheer physical security, the flowing luxury, of Orsino's court establishes an effective ideal, a locus of comfort towards which more confused characters may bend. And indeed, at the end of Viola's first scene, it is towards Orsino's court that she finds herself turning as though obeying an unconscious but unavoidable impulse. In this way too, though Viola can without difficulty be seen as the play's protagonist – she certainly provides its moral and ethical standard – it is the powerful figure of Orsino, the noble duke of Illyria, who literally dominates the play. Viola is a kind of messenger from the play to the reader or spectator: while she has no success in persuading characters onstage to heed her, she manages the job of expressing her private mind in such a way as to include us in her way of seeing. In a way she functions as a 'feminine' Isabella who gets what she wants because she deserves it. Like Isabella, Viola is subject to the royal whim which happens here, as it does not in *Measure for Measure*, to coincide with her own. To consider a reversal of the order of the scenes, however, is to imagine a significantly different effect. Orsino, set against the tribulations of Viola's wet and turbulent entrance, would be perceived differently. Seen thus he would seem a trivial and secondary character, for his background would include not only courtly luxury, but Viola's dangerous plight.

The two scenes, juxtaposed as they are, invite further speculations about the dramatic prestige of their two chief actors. Being

he play's first speaker gives Orsino a powerful advantage. This is
no ordinary speech; it sounds a keynote for the play, and critical
ingenuity notwithstanding, it is the rare first-time reader or spectator who can perceive Orsino as a mere self-inflating sybarite. As
Anne Barton has remarked, 'the lovelorn Orsino is not a figure of
fun. Indeed, the verse he speaks at the beginning of the play is
seductively beautiful: intense, metaphoric, and imaginative'.[10]
That first speech does much more than reveal the fatuity of its
speaker's attitude; it reveals a man in control of his fellow men, a
man whose favour it is good to have, a man of self-assurance, deep
feeling, intelligence – a good, strong duke of his dominions. The
narrative element of this first scene flows spontaneously from the
speech: its purpose is to convey the information of Orsino's un-
returned love of Olivia and to make the point that he is as yet
unmarried while eager to change this state. This detail acquires
new significance in the scene which follows with Viola's remark
about him, 'He was a bachelor then' (I, ii, 29) thereby linking her
future to his in a way not yet known. Her determination to serve
Olivia is made in ignorance of Olivia's genuine indifference to the
duke, an indifference which becomes perceptible upon her first
appearance in scene five.

It is again through the narrative and its arrangement that questions involving the two protagonists are resolved. For before
Olivia's first appearance Viola and the Duke are shown together for
the first time. This conjunction of the two characters at this point in
the narrative is a most significant moment in the drama. The
scene intends, as Craik says, to launch 'the dramatic irony of their
future relationship, and [the Duke's] closing lines hint at its happy
conclusion and at the apparent logical impossibility of that conclusion'.[11] The narrative force of this scene (I, iv) resides in the
coincidence of a plethora of adumbrated possibilities. It is in this
sense a fulfilment, in most instances logical, of expectations which
have been raised earlier and it is also, simultaneously, the beginning of another episode in the drama. As we have noted, in the first
two scenes the Duke's appearance is more or less expository, a
scene without action or 'drama', while Viola's first appearance,
charged with action and movement, neatly fulfils the requirements
of the definition of an episode by its beginning, middle, and end.
Here, in scene iv, once again Viola is engaged in an episode of
considerable import while Orsino, yet again, and true to form, is
virtually immobile as he soothes his bruised heart by eloquent

murmurings. This scene commences with the foreordained appearance of Viola in man's attire in service of the Duke. Thus the
beginning, while anticipated, possesses the new and drastic condition of the play of a chief character publically, symbolically, and
actually denying herself. The scene concludes with the unhappy
aside in which Viola attempts to recover at least a part of that self by
describing the distance that lies between her new sworn duty and
her deepest but necessarily hidden desires. The end of the episode,
in other words, is Viola's acknowledgement of the contradiction in
which she has been caught. She is engaged, once more, in a
dynamic action: at the end of this scene she is forced to an act
against her own interests. Orsino the while remains himself,
magisterially dominant by his command of the space they occupy,
and speaking with the easy fluent air of one who is accustomed to
respect.

Of the thirty-four lines spoken after he enters, Orsino speaks
twenty seven. This is, of course, socially and politically appropriate, as Viola is not so much an interlocutor as a servant. The
effect of this relationship between them, however, is to reiterate the
fact of Orsino's sheer dominance of the drama, a dominance which,
as Craik points out, has already been asserted by the appearance in
the previous scene of Sir Andrew as a ludicrously unsuitable suitor
to the object of Orsino's affections.[12] But also, in microcosm, the
scene mirrors the effect of the actions of the first two scenes. For as
there the stately articulation of Orsino, grandly static, was followed
by the frantic planning and deciding of Viola, so here the two styles
are compressed into the space of one scene where they are brought
into the same realm of action. In bringing Orsino and Viola together
Shakespeare stresses their oppositeness of station and character
and their opposed functions of doing and being. By her disguise
the playwright has further emphasized the most essential of the
opposite qualities which she possesses, that of her sex. There is no
other woman in the play as profoundly and selfconsciously
feminine as Viola. For to look upon her onstage or to read her lines
is to be reminded not just of who she really is but of what she really
is. Her womanliness is stressed by her mere presence because her
disguise is so powerful an indicator of her identity. For, while the
disguise is designed to conceal her real self from those around her
on stage, to the audience it is a pressing and constant reminder of
that real self. Where disguise is transsexual it alludes, by definition,
as strongly to the concealed gender as to the identity of the real self.

Once it becomes a part of the action, that is, once the character is shown concealing his or her identity, the identity being concealed is the foremost fact about that character and overwhelms all other information.

Viola's disguise and her perception of a need of it point to yet another crucial manner in which the narrative impulses of the play position themselves around the alternating forms of static and dynamic action. There is a palpable dichotomy between the two modes of action, between doing and standing still. Those who stand still, like the Duke and Olivia, who enjoy the luxury of merely being themselves, are those with assured status and measureable authority over others. However, as Orsino enjoys comfort and security and is propelled by a desire to satisfy his appetite for love's fulfilment, Viola's world is fragmented, uncertain, and austere, and for her the bodily needs must be attended to first.

These narrative 'facts' about their states reflect a central irony in the drama which is highlighted by the parody of it in the narrative involving Malvolio. Power is weakness and weakness is power: the Duke is powerful and therefore does little that requires intestinal strength. Viola is weak and is therefore compelled to act and do with all the energy and courage she can muster. From the first, where she needs to make a rapid-fire series of decisions and commitments to major actions involving her future, Viola is constantly on the move in one way or another. She has adopted the role of a servant and is thus compelled to subject her will and energy to the will of another. At the end of their first appearance together Orsino grandly exits with an unwitting prophecy of the ending – 'Prosper well in this,/And thou shalt live as freely as thy lord/To call his fortune thine' (I, iv, 38–40) – while Viola is left confused and bereft of hope.

She has her commission and works to effect it; what follows, insofar as the story concerns Viola, is the series of conflicts and misunderstandings which lend such comic and tragic force to her tale. The Duke meanwhile is seen only once more before the last scene. Yet his presence, his dominance, and strength are felt throughout, implicit as they are in the pursuits and difficulties of Viola. Indeed, as the Duke is implicit in the comic and serious scenes involving Viola, and as her purpose and her plight are reminders of his presence in the scheme of the drama, so Viola's presence is implicit in the person of Olivia once she has beheld her as Cesario. In this sense, that is, in the sense that the characters are seen to be moving from and towards each other, the characters in the play imply each other all of the time. So that even in such passages when they are absent from the stage, they are present in mind and link to one another continuously.

The irony persists. When the Duke is next seen, nothing has changed; the aura of stability which is denied by his assertions but so beautifully supplied by his balanced style, remains. His power is his basis in sureness and renders him immobile and, ultimately, inconstant or weak in feeling as he switches affections in a trice. But here we observe him yet again, a calm commanding figure surrounded by signs of his strength and enfeebled by them. He doesn't *have* to do anything. He can afford the luxury of publically displaying his private passion.

> For such as I am, all true lovers are,
> Unstaid and skittish in all motions else
> Save in the constant image of the creature
> That is belov'd.

(II, iv, 17–20)

The self-perception contained in this passage seems to be the precise reversal of the truth. Indeed, Orsino is constant and predictable in every motion save that of love, where, as we later learn, he is unstaid and skittish in the extreme. Again we are force to observe the conflict of Viola's silent but truly powerful emotions with their ironic expression by the Duke. Again we see Viola suppressing her love for an Orsino who presumes to lecture her upon the subject. And here too is repeated the pattern of hidden power in a tug-of-war with actual power. This, like those earlier scenes in which Viola and the Duke appear side by side or together, offers yet another episode in which the Duke relaxedly orders his world with no more effort than it takes him to breathe the words by which it is done. His sheer self-bolstering delight is manifest in his every word. He bemoans his fate, he interests himself in Cesario's, he directs, designs, and designates. The alternative is provided by Viola who is observed, interrogated, and ordered into action. Yet, despite this evidence of her lack of power, of her weakness of station, it is she whose words carry force, it is her sentiments that move us. To Viola we have been taught to look for the moral emotional truths around which the play revolves. Viola's public statement of her innermost secrets – which naturally remain secret while she is disguised – speak of the heartbreak of love and the power with which it can endure a determined spirit. So, the image created by the stage spectacle is realized: little Cesario, the affectionate Duke's plaything, is the repository of the real strength of love. Thus, the character of the scene, its emotional tension and its power to move or change the course of the play's events, resides not in the strong handsome Duke of Illyria, but in Viola. She is capable of removing her disguise at any time, and so tormented is her soul by the work she has to do and by the blindness of the man she loves that the temptation to remove it and to stop having to endure the torments enforced upon her is a possibility with which we have continuously to reckon, forewarned as we are that the resolution of the play is contingent upon just such an act. This scene offers a repetition of the pattern of that first appearance of Viola and Orsino together. It commences with her continuing helplessness in advancing his quest and it concludes with her being sent upon the same futile errand. Authority has asserted itself once again.

It is in this matter of authority that we find the basis of the parody of the values of the main plot comically asserted and reconstituted in the plot revolving around Malvolio and Olivia and her household. As Alvin Kernan has pointed out, authority over Oliva's household 'has appropriately passed into the hands of the puritanical and utterly self-centred Malvolio, and the over-repressed primal appetites, instead of being controlled and ordered, explode into the misrule and riot of . . . two carousing idiots'.[13] But, of course, Malvolio's authority is a delusion, his power is merely the gift of idleness to ambition; it is temporary and uncertain. Olivia, like Orsino, is immobilised in the performance of anything but the merest form of duty or work. Languishing, like Orsino, in a fog of ennui which she pleases to call grief as he pleases to call it love, she has handed over the power of *doing*, that is, of regulating and ordering her life, to another and lesser creature. Her occupation is hedged with triviality. But Malvolio's mode of activity is significantly different from and alternative to Viola's. For where she acts in another's behalf, Malvolio, the embodiment of austere self-promoting ambitiousness, acts only for himself. He is like Viola in his relation to his employer, but he is simultaneously a travesty of the unselfish ideal for which she stands. In Olivia's household the power structure has been superficially inverted and Malvolio has allowed himself to aspire on the basis of the semblance of power he enjoys, measuring this power in terms of the amount of activity he is assigned. That the inversion of authority is more in Malvolio's mind than in fact is evident early in the scene where Olivia addresses him with a forthright condemnation of his image of that public and evident self by which he wields authority:

> O, you are sick of self-love, Malvolio, and taste with distempered appetite. To be generous, guiltless, and of free disposition, is to take those things for bird-bolts that you deem cannon-bullets.

> (I, v, 89–93)

Thus are characters and their relationships revealed. And indeed fully half of his longish scene is devoted to merely revealing Olivia's household. The active narrative of the scene, however, centers upon the meeting of Viola and Olivia, and, incidentally, the high-lighting of the similarity of the roles of Viola and Malvolio. For it is Malvolio whom Olivia sends to repel and then admit Viola, and, at the end of the scene, she sends him with her ring in order to get Cesario to return. Thus Malvolio, like Cesario, is forced into the ill-fitting mould of Cupid's messenger. For both Olivia and Viola is their first meeting a crisis; as such it forms a crucial part of the narrative. For Viola the crisis is the more searing in that it provides the discovery that her rival in love is enviably beautiful. But she remains trapped all the same by her disguise. For Olivia, on the other hand the meeting provides a kind of liberation in the dis-covery of love. The past with its constraints and habits is abruptly dislocated as her heart fills with new sensations of unknown emotions and uncertain possibilities:

> I do I know not what, and fear to find
> Mine eye too great a flatterer for my mind.
> Fate show thy force! Ourselves we do not owe.
> What is decreed must be – and be this so!

> (I, v, 312–5)

Thus it is in his prison that Malvolio in dark parody most resembles Viola. Here, in what Alexander Leggatt describes as the play's 'most vivid image of the trapped isolated self',[14] is the matter of lonely unfulfilled love most completely realized. The scene, as eggatt notes, is 'almost an emblematic one, with Malvolio . . . educed to a crying voice'.[15] And indeed the scene is emblematic only because it 'stands for' the lovers in the play in their starkest despair. That voice of desperation is a shrill parody of the ironic voice of Viola in her disguised persona; it is the voice of the Orsino whom Orsino describes himself to be; it is the voice of Olivia remulously fearful to find her eye 'too great a flatterer' for her mind. Malvolio's anguished and uncomprehending voice is the voice too of the anonymous lover 'slain by a fair cruel maid' (II, iv, 4) in the Clown's sad and wistful song. All love in this play is reduced to and rescued from some form of incomprehensible pain whose source is that love whose source is unknowable in any ultimate terms. Thus, though the plot against Malvolio may well be, as John Hollander has suggested, to 'let him surfeit on himself',[16] and its purpose to feast him upon 'a vision of himself spread before him',[17] we are brought back time and again in the play, through its multiplicity of masks and mirrors and through its convolutions of story and narrative design to the single separate self of each character facing, in his own private and individual way, a vision of himself upon which he must feast or from which he must turn. Malvolio's case is thus merely the most explicitly and bluntly described, his pain and grief merely the most measurable, its source the readiest to hand. We and his enemies may reasonably charge him with gross ambition and love of a purely fantastic image of himself, less complexly poetic than Orsino's and less complexly self-conscious. But, what Shakespeare impresses upon our minds is less the unlikeness of Malvolio to those other selves of which the narrative is comprised than the way in which it contains them iconographically. Malvolio's situation is readily explicable in terms of the feelings he inspires in others, and of the way in which his tale possesses a neatly separable little morally and emotionally completed narrative of its own. As the tragic mask with its grotesque and exaggerated image of the sheerest human pain may be said to stand for and imply all tragedies, all of the sordid and terrible suffering that all tragedies contain, so Malvolio, reduced to an essential expression of his incorporeal self by mere uncomprehending sound, stands for all of the lonely questing selves in the drama.

Writing about *Hamlet*, Francis Ferguson has made the point that the Player King presents 'very pithily the basic vision of human action in the play, at a level so deep that it applies to all the characters: the guilty, the free, the principals, the bystanders, those

in power and the dispossessed'.[18] In the same way the 'basic vision
of *Twelfth Night* is presented through the torture and incomprehension of Malvolio whose plight is in an abstract sense the logical
concatenation or conclusion of the various and many stories of love
upon which the play depends. And here, in the spectacle of the
helpless steward being tormented by his enemies is the image of
doing and standing still most vividly realized: helplessness, so
rifely in evidence in each of the play's entanglements, is brought
face to face with dynamic opposition. The narrative thread, with its
dichotomizing of characters along lines of active or passive apprehension of the tribulations of love, is resolved through the exploitation of dramatic conventions, but the symbolic heart of the play
its objective correlative, affords no lasting resolution: the pain of
love will not go away, though it may be allayed. Thus Malvolio's
departure is a powerful reminder of his presence even after he is
gone. He remains with us and with those onstage in the same way
that the departure of Shylock cannot itself remove him from the
minds of those who have seen him depart. The thing which
Malvolio stood for in the play, the generalized assertion of love's
marriage to unhappiness must linger on, even as the embodiment
of that assertion is banished from the orderly presence of love's
requital. For Malvolio's departure is accompanied by his threat of
future vengeance; and it is a vengeance applicable not only to his
enemies but to all those who have seen his humiliation, Viola and
Sebastian no less than Sir Toby and Feste. Malvolio's exit is accompanied by a suggestion of violence. It is his last and perhaps most
characteristic act in the drama. His sin has been the desire to change
the world, to suppress its instinctual music and revelry. At the same
time he secretly and hypocritically hankers for its gifts for himself –
for riches, power, and idle luxury:

> Having been three months married to her, sitting in my state –
> (ii, v, 45) . . . Calling my officers about me, in my branch'd
> velvet gown; having come from a daybed, where I have left
> Olivia sleeping –   (II, v, 47–9)

His threat, then, is a threat to return and to do what he sought to do
in the first place, to impose his will on the world, to extirpate
pleasure after all, and destroy the manifest and the mysterious joys
of that world which the other characters seek. In storming from the

stage he reveals most clearly the way in which he differs from Viola, however much his role may have resembled hers and however much his fantasies have resembled hers in their removes from likely realization. Malvolio threatens revenge because he cannot accept his state, not even after his humiliation. Viola, on the other hand, accepts what happens to her and what she sees as her lot without the slightest struggle or attempt to determine a new direction for herself. Her acting in the play has been in the service of another, and her deliberate actions have been necessary or merely 'womanly' acts of submission of will to existing facts and circumstances. But, though she is submissive, Viola is unlike Malvolio in that she is wise about herself and in touch with her world. It is this wisdom that protects her from the possibilities of social disaster. Her contrary desires, unlike Malvolio's which they resemble in her love of her employer, are kept in check by her self-knowledge and her circumstances. Though intimately engaged in the events as they unfold, and while responsible both knowingly and unwittingly for the advancement of the narrative, Viola is nevertheless a watcher. Much of her time onstage is spent in commenting on the actions before her, in interpreting them and considering their effects upon herself. In this way she contains and constantly implies her various personae. But she does this with the kind of awareness of these alternative personae that is denied the others of the drama. We are aware of the ironies and duplicities of the personae of Orsino, Olivia, Malvolio, and even the buffoons. But they are not aware of them. Viola's disguise, however, is an indicator to herself of the doubleness of her self. She is constantly being forced by the alternative possibilities implied by the narrative in which she is engaged to note and expatiate upon the separation of her self into at least two parts.

The anomaly in the midst of all of this doubleness, at the still centre of the alternating and alternative narratives of this drama, is of course, Feste. Viola is a watcher, but only in part, being directly engaged in the events as they unfold. Her love places her heart squarely into the centre of the play's turmoil. The real watcher of the play is the clown. He is its centre of consciousness, its remote and objective mind, essentially disinvolved in the major actions and emotions which the dramas of the play generate. He is, as Ruth Nevo has said, 'the most detached, observant . . . and ironic of Shakespeare's fools, and the tutelary spirit of a play whose fooling is as serious as it is funny'.[19] The clown is compulsively and profes-

sionally wise and witty. He is incapable of letting down his guard
for his wit is his protection from this world: it is his garb and his
livelihood. So Feste is but one thing in the course of the play. He is
merely and completely the fool who knows. Feste's encounter with
Viola has little or no effect on the direction of the narrative. It
stands, however, as a strong symbolic moment in the play, for here
Viola's disguise for the only time is irrelevant to the dialogue. What
matters for the audience is that Feste's encounter with Viola has
little or no effect on the direction of the narrative. What matters here
for the audience is the first encounter of two characters who each
stand for a different aspect of the experience of the play. These are
the only two characters who know themselves and others in the
play, the only two characters in whom it is possible to place faith
And this is acknowledged by each of the other. Viola notes of Feste
that he is 'wise enough to play the fool', (III, i, 61) while Feste in a
characteristic pun tells her, 'I think I saw your wisdom there [at
Count Orsino's]' (III, i, 43). In his dialogue with Viola, Feste notes
of this world, that in it 'words are grown so false I am loath to have
to prove reason with them' (III, i, 24). He is alluding not only to the
duplicity of the world or to the propensity of its inhabitants to
deceive themselves with their fine speeches, but to a view of that
larger thing, the human necessity in Illyria to split oneself to one's
root as means of surviving. Thus he says somewhat ruefully or
bitterly of himself, that, 'I am indeed not her fool, but her corrupter
of words' (III, i, 36).

Feste's power as the mediator between the severed individuals
and selves of which the play is comprised is nowhere so evident as
in the ending of the play. There, all energy spent, the drama over,
the reader is offered the spectacle of the clown alone onstage in final
control of the play. His song, which follows the rituals of pairing
and expulsion by which the loves and animosities are resolved,
stands as a last emblem of the healed single self, alone, isolated
even, yet complete. For this song contains and overarches all of the
actions that have just passed. Orsino, the figure of power through
the play, seems to have handed over his sceptre to Feste who
reduces all the human activity which has occurred to the timeless
perspective of repeated patterns. The 'I' of the song is all men and all
women; those of the play and those of the world. The sufficiency
and wholeness of Feste's self give him the power to stand aside
from the action and to judge it. Yet the song, with its tragic image of
loneliness, stands for him as well. Having risked nothing, he has

lost nothing and gained nothing – his world is as it was. Yet his words and his material aloneness onstage seem to hold out the possibility that the happiness of the lovers, ephemeral though it may be, is better to possess than the wisdom which recognizes that it is ephemeral.

6   Modes of Story-Telling in *Othello*

The matter of Othello's competence has been at the centre of many long-standing discussions of his character.[1] To some critics he is above all the 'noble Moor', grand, dark, mysterious.[2] Other critics, usually reluctant to declare their outright hostility to him are, nevertheless, aware of a kind of failure of imagination and intelligence. Bradley himself noted, as A. D. Nuttall reminds us, that 'if the heroes of *Hamlet* and *Othello* change places, each play ends very quickly. Hamlet would see through Iago in the first five minutes and be parodying him in the next'.[3] William Empson noted that it is reasonable to complain that Othello was stupid to be deceived,[4] and more recently, Michael Long has alluded to the question of Othello's failure of comprehension in remarking the 'pained irritation' which is a strong component of our feelings at many points in the play.[5] In referring to Othello's incompetence I do not use the word to suggest any moral or, for that matter, intellectual weakness in Othello; rather I am referring to a reason for his vulnerability. It seems to me that in addition to the cultural questions, a major cause of Othello's destruction is the absence in him of a sense of the reciprocal movement between past and present; that in recalling his past Othello represents it as closed system, only tenuously connected to the present; that when he tries to make these connections he displays what Catherine Shaw calls his 'dangerous vulnerability'[6] most obviously. By contrast, Iago's success derives largely from his competence, a quality most vividly demonstrated in the brawl scene as he is made to develop connections between an audience-observed past event and the subsequent story by which it takes form.

Othello's vulnerability derives directly from his love of Desdemona, from a genuine and frequently expressed fear of its fragility which is too well known to need rehearsing here, but which, it may be noted, reveals a kind of terror of the present and the future, of that time *when* he has ceased to love Desdemona and chaos has

:ome again. Othello's method of coping with his fear seems to be to urn to the past where, by virtue of the inevitable and, even, :ompulsive human process by which the past is transmogrified nto narratives or stories, he can establish and demonstrate control over events which were once merely a part of the inchoate mass of daily experience. The past is a place where Othello seems to feel safe and, rather than being a backward extension of the present, is separated from it. Othello represents himself as two separate selves, the one a completed entity, the man he was, the other, more fragile self, is the man of the present. Facing challenges and resistance in the play, he frequently attempts to resolve the contradiction between the selves by a recreation of his old self, but seems unable to bring the old self into alignment with the present self.

Thus, it seems to me, that Eliot was essentially correct when he asserted that in his final speech Othello is *'cheering himself up*. He is endeavouring to escape reality'.[7] Indeed, in that last speech Othello is endeavouring to escape, but not so much from reality as from the present time, into that enclosed safe world where reality has been completed. We, audiences and readers, being wiser than Othello – and less wrought – can recognize in the habits of mind which determine the shape, tone and contents of that final speech, the hallmarks and modes of the speaker: we see Othello recreating his most competent self, artfully and feelingly telling a story from his past which for the first time successfully brings that past into the present with the devastating blow accompanying the final phrase, 'And smote him thus' (V, ii, 357). To describe this speech as 'self dramatizing' as Leavis has done, thus seems to me somewhat unkind.[8] Othello is searching for himself with an intensity and pain that deserve greater compassion than the epithet allows in any of its forms. One cannot, however, but recognize an element of truth in this description and that of Jane Adamson, who notes the way in which the characters of the play 'make up cheering stories about themselves or project images of themselves, stories and self-images tailored to fit the way they wish or need to see their lives'.[9]

Othello is deceived very largely about the nature of story-telling. His descriptions of his past take traditional narrative forms without acknowledging or recognizing that the narrator, by the mere fact of giving structure to an event, by the act of articulation, automatically fictionalizes it, however, 'true to life' it may be. Once the narrative form possesses the event, once it becomes subject to the inevitable process of selection and reduction, it becomes a fiction. Othello insists from the first that he always speaks the literal truth, that his exemplary mode is the 'round unvarnish'd tale' (I, iii, 90). Yet, of course, his speeches, with their unerring sense of the dramatic, are replete with the adornments of a refulgent rhetoric which demonstrate a master story-teller at work. As Derick Marsh has observed, 'it is quite remarkable how little we know of what Othello has felt, as opposed to what he has done, beyond what he has endured'.[10] His past life is represented as a multiplicity of heroic and interesting incidents calculated to establish his exoticism and difference from other men. In his account of his courtship of Desdemona to the senate, Othello is given strength by his mastery of the mode of fiction. The significance of the Duke's statement that the 'tale' (I, iii, 171) would have the power to win his own daughter lies in its double-edged recognition that while the senate has been regaled with an autobiography of seductive magnificence, the autobiography may also be a tale in the sense, current in the sixteenth century, of 'a mere story, as opposed to a narrative of fact; a fiction, an idle tale; a falsehood' (*OED*). The Duke interestingly separates the teller from his tale, not admitting that Othello would win his daughter but that his *tale* would. The selectively reordered past provides Othello with the convenient means to reconstitute the present self in a flawless form by reliance on the depiction of a past and absent self. Noting the self-aggrandising quality of this self depiction, Barbara Everett observes that behind the account of Othello's travels and battles, 'there lies the braggart's invariable evocation of the grandeur of his battles and campaigns'.[11] From Othello's first speech in the play we can adduce the motive of vanity and its hidden face, insecurity, as partial explanations of the fulsome phrases of self-elevation by which he proclaims himself in the face of the threat of present circumstances:

> . . . tis yet to know –
> Which when I know that boasting is an honour,
> I shall provulgate – I fetch my life and being
> From men of royal siege; and my demerits
> May speak unbonneted to as proud a fortune
> As this that I have reach'd.

> (I, ii, 18–23)

Before the audience of the senate Othello's story-telling mode reveals itself clearly. There is a perceptible process of 'othering' as Othello describes himself as an entity quite separated from the man who is speaking the words. The separation is evident in the completeness of the narrative. The story of his past becomes a neatly encapsulate whole which entirely contains that other. That is, the persona of the past is given an existence as complete as that of a character in a story engaged in a series of heroic encounters. The connection between the speaker and the 'I' of the story is attenuated by the absence of remembered or described feeling as noted by Marsh. The ulterior purpose of this narrative is of course a factor in its composition. Othello wishes to convince the senators of Venice that he – an apparently inappropriate suitor to the most sought-after virgin of Venice – is also that other character who is the hero of his narrative. As a story, the speech is a masterpiece with its concise and eloquent reaching after the high moments of an inherently exciting life. It bears the stamp of being often told – indeed it has been told at least twice before, its grand details sufficiently fleshed out, perhaps, to have won from his favourite auditor a world of sighs. It was told to Brabantio in the hearing of Desdemona who subsequently begged for and, presumably, received a second hearing. The story is burnished from polishing and refining, both inevitable by-products of its retelling. Thus, while it is surely unfair to call this narrative a lie, it is still, in a sense, a kind of half-truth simply by virtue of the facts of its form and style. His life, he here claims, consists of one shocking adversity upon another: for while he asserts that the story of his life from year to year consists of battles, sieges, and fortunes, we must note that the fortunes play almost no part in the story: it concentrates on that which is likelier to win sympathy – his accidents and scapes.

Othello has become thoroughly identified with this speech. For most, it is profoundly romantic with its mood of exotic heroism and its capacity to conjure up the fantasm of experience and knowledge of a stranger life than any who hear it can know. It tells a sorrowful but brave history of anguish and suffering which its speaker masks as the mere means of an unusual growing up. The story tantalizes its auditors by its necessary omission of the details of horrendous events and spectacles which are redeemed only by the fact that the victim of the suffering which it describes is present and recounting it: that is, it has a happy ending. In its simple phrases are distilled oceans of experience and pain: 'And sold to slavery and my redemption thence' (I, iii, 138). While the putative purpose of the speech is to address the matter of how Othello made Desdemona fall in love with and marry him without her father's consent, its real function is an existential justification. The major achievement of the speech, however, lies not in its tone or language, but rather in its splendid defiance: Othello does not claim, like Demetrius arguing his suitability for Hermia, that he is a proper husband for Desdemona because he meets some bourgeois requirements valued by the society he addresses himself to. Instead he emphasizes his differences from that society as the basis of his claim. In a sense, he exploits his blackness as an advantage. His world is the remote and unfamiliar, and he proudly notes these aspects of his life. The qualities of this and other of his speeches, however, which most eloquently argue his present suitability as Desdemona's husband are the spontaneity of his cultural signifiers of the society of his adoption. Reuben Brower has pointed out the 'Latin intricacy of Othello's syntax',[12] and Howard Felperin discusses Othello's 'wholehearted adoption of the dramatic vocabulary of Christian allegory [which] projects his essential relation to the Venetian society that [Desdemona] represents'.[13]

Othello's speech at the end of the play, the one which Nuttall identifies has having caused the most trouble,[14] brings to a resolution the past and present selves as represented through stories with the single concluding word, 'thus'. And yet, as has been noted, it is similar in many ways to the senate speech. Where in the early speech we have aggrandisement of the past self, almost casual confidence, an aura of vanity rich as cream, in the last speech we have the simple opposites of these qualities, humility, self-abasement, a bottomless self loathing. And it is not until the enunciation of that last 'thus' that we are enabled to note, despite the rapid descent from self-love to murderous self-disgust, that a meliorating awareness has been achieved between the two major phases.

With the 'thus' in our minds we may with hindsight begin to recognize in the last speech an expansion of awareness and a concomitant acquisition of the knowledge of the nature of the evil within the self which have the effect of infusing the hero with a palpable sense of his own capacity for moral ugliness.

The greatest likeness between the two speeches is in the way both take the form of stories of fictional recreations of a past life involving that other Othello not at first immediately or recognizably connected with the present speaker. While Giorgio

Melchiori's assertion that this last speech constitutes a recovery of Othello's 'real' self strikes me as somewhat simplistic in its assumptions about what Othello's real self is, he is surely correct in pointing out the similarity of the rhetorical patterns displayed in the two passages.[15] In the early speech Othello presents a potently glorifying view of his past self; he reaches back into his past and plucks out only gold. But when his present joy lies slain, when the present has asserted its dominance over that history by its encroaching nearness and looming magnitude, so does the entire past reveal itself to him as another more diffuse element. Now, as his last speech shows, the present mood is entangled not only with the horror of Desdemona's murder, but also with the memory of other murders, of other acts in Othello's past whose once forgotten or neglected role was to dim its glory. In Othello's story in the senate there are no malignant Turks; those who enslaved him are realized only as agents of his greatness. The details of the early narrative contain only two visible participants, himself and Desdemona. Behind them exists a shadowy multitude who constitute the means through which the lovers are united. The Anthropophagi and cannibals who populate this world of shadows intensify the atmosphere of story against whose background the most clearly delineated object is the hero of his own tale. This sense of indefiniteness of background has been remarked by R. A. Foakes who points out that Othello 'does not say he has *seen* cannibals or Anthropophagi but he claims authority in talking about them', and that something of the 'fabulous . . . may be thought of as transferring to him'.[16]

But in the last narrative there intrudes another figure, not at all vaguely drawn: here is the precisely delineated infidel (turbanned, circumcised, vocal) here it is he, the other, who has been the victim. Moreover, in the reflection of this dark malignant figure, Othello's personal symbol of treachery, Othello acknowledges an undisclosed aspect of himself. That he should note, from inference in all probability, that his victim was circumcised is an atavistic jolt by which self-loathing is carried to a furious pitch. For as Othello himself must be circumcised, and as that sacramental rite by which he must once have been bound to another faith relates directly to sexuality and the sexual devastation of the play, so in the moment of the oath he becomes the dog of his description, a traitor to Desdemona, to Venice, to Christianity, *and* to his first faith. Nuttall notes that stabbing himself, Othello in a 'horrific parallelism . . .

as if a last act of devoted service, his last propitiatory offering to the state, . . . kills the outsider, Othello'.[17] Stabbing himself, Othello becomes his own victim: the past, once so useful is useful again, as a self-enclosed system, now reorganized along lines appropriate to present circumstances. This, the last story, is no more true or false than the romantic narratives which precede it; selected simply from different zones of his history, it is quite as much a reductive fiction. In this story, as in that told to the senate, Othello seems driven to expose himself, to tell his story before an audience. With the final act of stabbing himself upon the word 'thus', Othello seems to show his recognition of the connection between the two Othellos who dominate his world – the historic other self and the present evident self. With the word-accompanied act there is a conflation of the separate selves as the teller becomes both the murderer and his victim in the story, providing the conclusion by literally entering the action of the tale. In doing this, Othello actively synthesises time, place and action: the past and the present, the other place and this place, the other self and this present self are united.

In his last narrative Othello has reversed his role. Brower argues that the process of 'swinging from one state to its opposite . . . is very characteristic of him'.[18] There is a progression towards the irreversible and absolute truth of the act of self murder that provides the speech with its climax. From self-pity – 'not wisely, but too well' (V, ii, 345) – to a recognition of folly – 'Threw a pearl away' (348) – to an awareness of pain – 'Drops tears as fast as the Arabian tree' (351) – and, finally, to a deadly anger against his fictional and his present and real selves. Characteristically, in this speech, Othello moves away from the present time and place. He takes himself to an Eastern, pagan world of the past, as in the senate speech. What Lawrence Danson describes as 'the hectic language of jealousy and hate'[19] and the chaotic emotions they express have been subjugated to a controlled tongue: the rhythm of the 'Othello music'[20] has been restored, but the melody is deadly solemn. Order in Othello's words is no longer synonymous with light and love alone. Instead, a searing hatred of himself is expressed. His vanity, converted to self disgust, the destruction is completed by the blow whose force allows him to revive a single meliorative memory from a destroyed past life, the only *cheering* detail transformed into a remembered narrative and winnowed from a past now turned to ashes. The last words, like the blow at himself, bring the two times in which he lived successfully and unsuccessfully into a magnifient conjunction. 'I kiss'd thee ere I kill'd thee, no way but this' 359) is a story, 'Killing myself, to die upon a kiss' (360) brings the tory dynamically into the present.

Between these two opposing evocations of the past lies the tranitional sacrifice speech which plays a vital function in preparing Othello for the final reconciliation of his self-created personae. The ictions of the scene are structured in such a way as to provide the pposing modes of the self-contained story and the present reality vith visible and articulated forms. The sacrifice speech represents he testing moment of decision for the hero of his stories. It is one hing to determine in Iago's presence – and fed by Iago's suggesions – to kill Desdemona, but it is another to perform the deed itself n private, for privacy and a sleeping wife allow no audience outide the self. In the two speeches already mentioned, Othello lemonstrates a clear and simple historical perspective by which he educes his actions, through the narrative mode, from universal to personal significance; they have, that is, social magnitude as well a ourely personal meaning. In the sacrifice speech, however, Othello's purpose is to persuade only himself of the rightness of his ntention. But, deprived of an audience, he is deprived of the need or a story form. He needs to understand for himself alone that the hing must be done for its own sake: the apparatus of fiction is rrelevant. Confronted by the fact of what he means to do and the physical reality of the deed in the form of his sleeping wife, he orces himself to face the present reality of his act. The moods and enses of the speech signify the changes in him. 'It is the cause' (V, i, 1) firmly plants the deed into a continuous present. Other moods, imperatives, subjunctives, and futures, testify to his determination to see clearly both the act and its consequences. Where at other times he can take refuge in the organized and closed past, here he faces only the present and the future. While the discourse of he passage may be morally clear, it does, nevertheless, demonstrate damning moral limitations and also how the habit of self-deception clings to him. Brian Vickers declares that this speech, with its marvelously wrought language, a ceremony that Othello hinks of as a sacrifice, is the most fictitious scene in Shakespeare – not a word in it that Othello says is true'.[21] The crux of the speech is he hideously self-deceiving statement that Desdemona 'must die, else she'll betray more men (V, ii, 6). Around this stunning equation can he really think that he is killing his wife for the sake of Cassio's successors in Desdemona's bed?) Shakespeare has constructed a

speech of breathtaking beauty which invokes and challenges the
eternal verity of the triumph of death over life. But, lingering in the
back of the mind of the reader or spectator, throughout the exquisitely painful realizations given such lyrical voice, there always
remains the memory of that false rationalization, a violent contradiction of the brutal realism by which he has been brought to this
lyricism. That he utters the banality at all, alludes to his normal
human need to understand the impulses of his emotions in rational
terms and to attribute reasonable motives to an act of passion. But
the statement sticks there in the core of the speech, a testimony to
his dependence upon the self of his stories. That is, the Othello of
Othello's heroic memory is not a man to sacrifice his wife for selfish
motives, *he* does so for the sake of others for his world.

The confusion, later in the scene of murder and sacrifice – which
we may take to be the playwright's reminder to us that we are
witnessing murder – takes an added poignancy as the self image of
Othello becomes mangled by present reality. Thus does the drama
demonstrate the inescapable presence of the past. While Othello
does not in this speech create or recall a second historic self as so
often elsewhere, that old self is evident in each line. The presence of
an articulated motive is a terrible but central anomaly as it successfully distorts the tone of the entire passage. For all its self-conscious
universalism, it remains a devastatingly personal and self-serving
statement. In a speech that strikes at the heart of human fears about
death and, more dangerously, about the human capacity to take
life, this line of extenuation fails to relate Othello to his deed or to
Desdemona. It reveals its falsity by the adoption of a tone not suited
to that of the whole: it refers back to a system of values which have
no relevance to the situation. Othello's voice is the voice of justice
and the law; the delicate and fragile anguish of the words before
and after the line are traduced by the exculpation and, even more,
by the speaker's obvious need for exculpation. Othello kills Desdemona because he believes in his heart that she has betrayed him
and he knows that she has wounded him. He kills her because she
had made him a fool. Despite the calm of the speech, he finally kills
her from a rage that only the deepest kind of passionate hurt can
produce: the carefully nurtured image of his story self has been
broken, and he seems to believe that by killing Desdemona he can
expunge his rage and its cause. The speech is a deliberate and
self-conscious attempt to restore his remembered self.

Where in his stories Othello separates himself from his present, so here he attempts to acquire emotional control by separating himself from Desdemona. Not once does he refer to her as his wife or by her name. She is 'you' and 'she', transformed into a scapegoat of ritual killing, an object into which the transgressions and violations of social and sacred codes have been concentrated. In this sense, 'else she'll betray more men' becomes comprehensible as Othello takes upon himself the pointedly dramatic role of priest or ritual slaughterer whose killing is a socially acceptable means by which the value of marital fidelity is restated, reaffirmed and resanctified for society. But, by waking and speaking, Desdemona abruptly destroys the fictional objectified personae her husband has made of himself and her. She reminds him with the force of her humanity of who and what she is. From this sudden reconstruction of the bases of his fiction issues Othello's anguished cry, 'thou dost stone thy heart/And makest me call what I intend to do/A murder which I thought a sacrifice' (V, ii, 64–6). As she slept he had evaded by his fictionalization of their roles the fact of Desdemona's humanity. Her voice – her present and evident reality – recalls it to him. For while Desdemona sleeps, Othello is able to involve her with the inanimate objects around them; thus to de-personalize and de-individualize her by evasion and metaphor. Her life is like the flame of the candle, she becomes the living rose. This is not to argue that the emotions he expresses are not deeply felt but, rather, that the effort to diminish her reality succeeds through this perception of her as another object to be consigned to his world of story.

He is here facing the present just as he is retreating from it, suffusing the deed of murder with characteristically emotive grandiosity. He is shying away from the bestial present self that flashed out as it threatened to 'chop her into messes' (IV, i, 196) in the future, away from the motive of this act of revenge and hatred. What is most painful in Desdemona's murder is that because she wakes, the tumultuous, uncontrolled hatred of Othello is given occasion to surface; thus the real motives of the act cannot be stilled, and so he stifles his wife in a burst of abusive fury – 'Down, strumpet!' (V, ii, 80).

The present tenses and future imaginings of the sacrifice speech determine its differences from his stories. Those narratives in which Othello recollects his past life always address the question of his identity. In this speech, he is trying to place the whys and wherefores of his rage and present being into some kind of order.

What Othello means by 'It is the cause', as M. R. Ridley notes, 'is far from clear'.[22] But the recurrence of the phrase together with the speculative impulses it releases in the speech indicate a clear determination to perform an act dictated by the processes of reason and right. The speech does not search for reasons, it asseverates them as though they were clear, unchallengeable and axiomatic. It reflects the speaker's courage in its lucid awareness of the consequences of acting rightly. From his fury Othello has plucked a certain truth – 'she must die' – and upon this truth he constructs a self-deceiving, consolatory value system whose basis, 'else she'll betray more men' – is the cause. Yet he is too much the lover and too much the warrier not to know with crushing certainty what the logical process implies. Thus are consolation and the values from which it is derived rendered impotent or irrelevant in the face of the more cruel simple truth that 'when I have pluck'd the rose,/I cannot give it vital growth again' (V, ii, 13–14). And thus, implicitly, even in Othello's eyes, does Desdemona become an innocent. Her physical helplessness in this state renders her one with innocence itself: her life is his to extinguish or allow. This knowledge forces him to pause. Reason and consolation are endangered by the pause as the words he speaks bring him again and again perilously close to the surface of present reality. 'When *I* have pluck'd the rose . . . It must needs wither' (V, ii, 13–15) places the speaker in the centre of his speech, as does his deployment of most of the images: '*I* know not where is that Promethean heat/That can thy light relume' (V, ii, 12–13; my italics). But such images rise not, as earlier, from actual deeds and past experience so much as from the literary and imaginative history of the speaker, a major resource of his fictionalizing. Desdemona's awakening robs Othello of the orderliness of the story form. The Othello music is distorted by details which do not conform to the artist's planning and which the conventions of fiction normally allow him to abandon. The script, the story – Othello's noble sacrifice in this instance – is interrupted by human reality. The speech is an elaborate hymn to himself; one can easily imagine Othello's satisfaction had he destroyed Desdemona in her sleep. Then, we may guess, he would beautifully and nobly have slaughtered himself, satisfied that duty had been done. But life, Shakespeare seems to be insisting by waking Desdemona, is more complex than fiction and will not be so readily bound and gagged as rhapsodists like Othello seem to need to believe. The murder of Desdemona is an urgent and terrible thing, and Othello's attempts to define it as otherwise cannot be permitted to succeed in a drama so moralistic as this one. Shakespeare's larger fiction – the play itself – like Othello's smaller tales within it, possess its own pattern. Othello kills his wife against all planning, in horrible mad rage, at a moment when reason and sanity are so completely subsumed by jealous anguish that the mad self is acting out of compulsions which radically oppose that harmoniously-ordered story self which contrived the sacrifice.

As Othello finds himself most secure by leaning backwards into his past, Iago seldom refers to the life he led before he knew Othello. His sheer busyness, expressed in his need to plot and contrive and initiate activity and avoid danger are articulated in part by his attitude to time and his emphasis upon the demands of present reality as it determines future possibility. When talking of his recent past since he joined Othello, he usually employs an historic present tense to describe events. The habit is particularly evident in the first scene where to justify his hatred of Othello, Iago uses a present tense to lend his narrative the conviction and authenticity that description can acquire from hasty breathless phrasing: 'And in conclusion,/Nonsuits my mediators: for "Certes", says he,/I have already chosen my officer!' (I, i, 15–17). Time past is thus made vividly present. Comparing Iago's means of recalling the past with Othello's, we observe essential differences between them. Iago's narratives depend upon the dramatic and realistic presentation of detail; they are reflections of a busy, vividly active, everyday world. His method, as Empson remarks, is 'the "direct" way to work'.[23] This first retrospective speech brings the past into immediate relation to the present – in contradistinction to Othello – and is shown as the impulse which drives him to future action. He achieves his effect by vividly realised historic presents and the use of direct quotation, typical means by which the drama of realistic fiction is heightened.[24] Little in the play highlights the sheer familiar contemporaneity of Iago – and thus the strangeness of Othello by contrast – so much as the buzzing terrorism of the first scene with its raucously real and crudely farcical delineations.[25]

Iago's mode of directness which bodies forth in his speeches as scorching declarations of dangerous intent define the way in which he is Othello's antithesis. His bald assertions of hatred suggest that he is discomposed by the past. He lives in the present, brings the past forward to the moment of recreating it partly because in that past there seems to have been little but failure and threat. His statement, 'I do suspect the lustful Moor/Hath leap'd into my seat' (II, I, 290–1) possesses a past tense, yet the emphasis is placed upon his present suspicion and eschews the opportunity to dwell upon old experience. The past is a trap, containing professional disappointment and an unfaithful wife. It is as real as Othello's past, but replete with painful associations rather than satisfying and self-bolstering images.

Iago's competence resides in his almost total comprehension of the way Othello's mind works. He recognizes, among other things, Othello's dependence upon the fictional image of himself, which has been culled from his personal history. And he sees how Othello depends upon stories as a way of showing up the fragile present time. In his first complete narrative in the play, Iago creates a false past out of lies; by employing the techniques of the story form – to which Othello has shown himself so vulnerable – he produces a new, complete narrative from the past which is designed to rest uneasily with those Othello has constructed:

> I lay with Cassio lately,
> And being troubled with a raging tooth,
> I could not sleep.
> There are a kind of men so loose of soul,
> That in their sleeps will mutter their affairs,
> One of this kind is Cassio:
> In sleep I heard him say "Sweet Desdemona,
> Let us be wary, let us hide our loves';
> And then, sir, would he gripe and wring my hand,
> Cry out, 'Sweet creature!' and then kiss me hard,
> As if he pluck'd up kisses by the roots,
> That grew upon my lips, then laid his leg
> Over my thigh, and sigh'd, and kiss'd, and then
> Cried 'Cursed fate, that gave thee to the Moor!'

> (III, iii, 419–30)

The realism of the speech provides an illuminating contrast to Othello's stories. And it is the realism which makes it work as a piece of persuasion; which makes it so immediately believable. The speech is richly and precisely detailed, replete with direct speech. Its metaphoric line has cunningly effective concreteness – 'As if he pluck'd up kisses by the roots'. Until its utterance Othello fights a disposition to believe in Desdemona's treachery, but after Iago has filled his mind with the vivid picture of tangible completed acts he becomes convinced of Iago's truth. That is, the fiction and the form it takes strike a chord which Iago was not able to reach by inference and innuendo alone.

Having shown a fiction disrupted by life – the sacrifice and its consequence – and a fiction created out of air – Iago's account of Cassio's dream, Shakespeare then uses Iago to discredit and subvert the entire function and form of story-telling by providing us with an event and a wholly distorted but 'true' story of it. Iago is seen arranging the calamitous drunken brawl and then turning it skillfully into narrative form in such a way that throws into question the entire nature of narrative by which we are alternately seduced and repelled through the play. It is inarguable that the tale of the brawl, as Iago narrates it to Othello, possesses a kind of truth while being at the same time, only partially true. The details of Iago's relation are accurate, but they are selected and ordered to serve the ulterior motive of the narrator. Iago begins his story of the event with, 'Montano and myself being in speech' (II, iii, 216) and leaves out what observers may regard as that crucial beginning when he persuaded Cassio to drink against his better judgement. The point is not that Iago is lying, but that the story of an event which we witness in advance of its transformation into narrative is simultaneously true and false. The question of the reliability of all narratives inevitably arises. Iago knows clearly that matter is always 'minced', but not always for 'honesty and love' (II, iii, 238).

Iago's competence, as his narrative technique shows, lies largely in his powerful awareness of the connections of the past to the present and future. This awareness is made manifest in his relation of the story of the brawl. Here he creates a sense of the violence and chaos of the event we have just witnessed by bringing the action forward to the very moment in which it is being described: his adherence to the present tense is effective. 'Thus it is, general/ Montano and myself being in speech,/There comes a fellow, crying out for help' (II, iii, 215–17).

In the first scene of *Othello*, Iago utters an extenuation of the deceitful role he is compelled to play. He tells Roderigo that 'Though I do hate him, as I do hell's pains,/Yet for necessity of present life,/I must show out a flag, and sign of love' (I, i, 154–6). Present life is the dominating element of Iago's existence: it is concentrated with angry force into the phrase that most denotes him in the play, 'I am not what I am' (I, i, 65). Here the present tense and the monosyllabic power carry an aggressive confidence which characterize Iago almost throughout – what Empson has called his "honest dog" tone'.[26] It is a phrase that, for all its difficulty, is unmistakeably identified with Iago. As Othello becomes transformed by jealousy he becomes like Iago in his developing sense of the danger and urgency of present time and the perilousness of what is to come. The future becomes terrifying to him most obviously when the past, which he has tended to regard as a fixed, stable system, begins to change shape. When Iago tells Othello of Cassio's sleep-talking, Othello is suddenly made to know that he cannot control the present because his own past has been undermined by being linked to another's. That past, upon which he has so powerfully depended has come to threaten present comfort. In this newfound fear of the past, in this sense that action must come from hostility based upon that fear, Othello comes to resemble Iago, whose pursuit depends upon an antipathy to what has been and upon a consequent determination to mould the future into a shape that will transform the future-past into a story of success.

As Othello's self-perceptions are modified by circumstances, so do the horrors of the past – the imagined, the literary and the actual experiences – begin to pierce the calm surface of Othello's memory. Between the serene adjuration, 'Keep up your bright swords for the dew will rust 'em' (I, ii, 59) to the brutal moan, 'I see that nose of yours but not the dog I shall throw't to' (IV, i, 140) the imagination has made a mighty plummet. Yet it is convincingly the same imagination whose images stem from a vast encompassing experience of life. That the soldier's memory should include the tragic image of rusting swords and fallen soldiers is natural. That the same mind can discover in its past an ugly outcrop of murderous emotion, that such a mind can be capable of summoning pictures from a realm of evil cruelty, serves to extend the distance of the decline and to highlight hidden corners of the same personal history. Lines like these capture moments of spontaneous self-revelation more successfully and lead us to a clearer knowledge of the hero. The single sudden images are compulsive expressions of the self when it is neglecting the discipline of narratives.

It might be argued that, in a sense, Iago is even more self-dramatizing than Othello, though he is certainly not so dependent upon or separated from the drama of his history. Iago's public expression is hedged with the motive of maintaining his public image and keeping it separate from his private design. Unlike Othello, who tries to maintain the separateness of the two solitudes that make up his self, Iago recognizes his task to be to balance the two selves of his creation, a performance which ultimately finds true expression in his final declaration of future silence.

In the last words of Iago and Othello some of these aspects of their characters are expressed. Iago demonstrates impressive strength in his adumbration of a grim, short future. His words, alluding only to the present and future time, repeat in the attitude they contain and the tone in which they are delivered, his fearlessness of present and future, and his determination to remain to face them until he is dead. As he has seldom looked behind him in the course of the play, so here, at the end, he remains consistent. 'Demand me nothing, what you know, you know/From this time forth I never will speak word' (V, ii, 304–5). Othello, as true to himself, and as consistent, extracts a consolation for the present from his past. Reaching back in anguish, through the violence and evil of recent history, he finds a self-enhancing truth to die with, a detail from his past around which he once more constructs a tiny, but complete narrative, a remembered kiss.

7 Shylock and the Idea of the Jew

Current criticism notwithstanding, *The Merchant of Venice* seems to me a profoundly and crudely anti-Semitic play. The debate about its implications has usually been between inexpert Jewish readers and spectators who discern an anti-Semitic core and literary critics (many of them Jews) who defensively maintain that the Shakespearean subtlety of mind transcends anti-Semitism. The critics' arguments, by now familiar, center on the subject of Shylock's essential humanity, point to the imperfections of the Christians, and remind us that Shakespeare was writing in a period when there were so few Jews in England that it didn't matter anyway (or, alternatively, that because there were so few Jews in England Shakespeare had probably never met one, so he didn't really know what he was doing). Where I believe the defensive arguments go wrong is in their heavy concentration on the character of Shylock; they overlook the more encompassing attempt of the play to offer a total poetic image of the Jew. It is all very well for John Russell Brown to say *The Merchant of Venice* is not anti-Jewish, and that 'there are only two slurs on Jews in general';[1] but this kind of assertion, a common enough one in criticism of the play, cannot account for the fear and shame that Jewish audiences and readers have always felt from the moment of Shylock's entrance to his final exit. I wish to argue that these feelings are justified and that such an intuitive response is more natural than the critical sophistries whose purpose is to exonerate Shakespeare from the charge of anti-Semitism. Although few writers on the subject are prepared to concede as much, it is quite possible that Shakespeare didn't give a damn about Jews or about insulting England's minuscule Jewish community, and that, if he did finally humanize his Jew, he did so simply to enrich his drama. It is, of course, interesting to speculate on whether Shakespeare was an anti-Semite, but we cannot rise beyond speculation on this point.

The image of Jewishness which *The Merchant of Venice* presents is contrasted with the image of Christianity to which it is made referable and which ultimately encompasses and overwhelms it. Though it is simplistic to say that the play equates Jewishness with evil and Christianity with goodness, it is surely reasonable to see a moral relationship between the insistent equation of the *idea* of Jewishness with aquisitive and material values while the *idea* of Christianity is linked to the values of mercy and love. In this chapter I wish first of all to demonstrate that *The Merchant of Venice* is an anti-Semitic play by examining the image of Jewishness which it presents and by placing that image in the contrasting context of Christianity to which it is automatically made referable. Secondly, I wish to examine the paradox which follows from my assertion of the anti-Semitic nature of the play – that is, the way in which Shylock is humanized in his final scene and made simultaneously both the villain of the drama and its unfortunate victim.

Let us first ask what is meant by anti-Semitism when that term is applied to a work of art. Leo Kirschbaum suggests that it is a 'wholly irrational prejudice against Jews in general, noting it would be difficult to accuse any of the Christian characters in *The Merchant of Venice* of such a vice'.[2] This seems to be John Russell Brown's view as well; he perceives the play's only anti-Semitic remarks to be Launcelot's statement 'my master's a very Jew' (II, ii, 100) and Antonio's comment about Shylock's 'Jewish heart' (IV, i, 80).[3] While generally acceptable, Kirschbaum's definition seems to me to err in its use of the term irrational. Prejudice is almost always rationalized, and it is rationalized by reference to history and mythology. Jews have been hated for a number of reasons, the most potent among them that they were the killers of Jesus Christ.

I would define an anti-Semitic work of art as one that portrays Jews in a way that makes them objects of antipathy to readers and spectators – objects of scorn, hatred, laughter, or contempt. A careful balance is needed to advance this definition, since it might seem to preclude the possibility of an artist's presenting any Jewish character in negative terms without incurring the charge of anti-Semitism. Obviously, Jews must be allowed to have their faults in art as they do in life. In my view, a work of art becomes anti-Semitic not by virtue of its portrayal of an individual Jew in uncomplimentary terms but solely by its association of negative racial characteristics with the term Jewish or with Jewish characters generally. What we must do, then, is look at the way the word *Jew* is used and how Jews are portrayed in *The Merchant of Venice* as a whole.

The word *Jew* is used 58 times in *The Merchant of Venice*. Variants of the word like *Jewess, Jews, Jew's,* and *Jewish* are used 14 times. *Hebrew* is used twice. There are, then, 74 direct uses of *Jew* and unambiguously related words in the play. Since it will readily be acknowledged that Shakespeare understood the dramatic and rhetorical power of iteration, it must follow that there is a deliberate reason for the frequency of the word in the play. And as in all of Shakespeare's plays, the reason is to surround and inform the repeated term with associations which come more and more easily to mind as it is used. A word apparently used neutrally in the early moments of a play gains significance as it is used over and over; it becomes a term with connotations that infuse it with additional meaning.

The word *Jew* has no neutral connotations in drama. Unlike, say, the word *blood* in *Richard II* or *Macbeth* – where the connotations deepen in proportion not merely to the frequency with which the word is uttered but to the poetic significance of the passages in which it is employed – *Jew* has strongly negative implications in *The Merchant of Venice*. It is surely significant that Shylock is addressed as 'Shylock' only seventeen times in the play. On all other occasions he is called 'Jew' and is referred to as 'the Jew'. Even when he and Antonio are presumed to be on an equal footing, Shylock is referred to as the Jew while Antonio is referred to by name. For example, in the putatively disinterested letter written by the learned doctor Bellario to commend Balthazar/Portia, there is the phrase '*I acquainted him with the cause in controversy between the Jew and Antonio . . .*' (IV, i, 153–4). Similarly, in the court scene Portia calls Shylock by his name only twice; for the rest of the scene she calls him Jew to his face. The reason for this discrimination is, of course, to set Shylock apart from the other characters. This it successfully does. Calling the play's villain by a name which generalizes him while at the same time ostensibly defining his essence is, in a sense, to depersonalize him. As in our own daily life, where terms like *bourgeois, communist* and *fascist* conveniently efface the humanness and individuality of those to whom they are applied, the constant reference to Shylock's 'thingness' succeeds in depriving him of his humanity while it simultaneously justifies the hostility of his enemies. The word *Jew* has for centuries conjured up associations of foreignness in the minds of non-Jews. When it is epeatedly used with reference to the bloodthirsty villain of the play, its intention is unmistakable. And the more often it is used, he more difficult it becomes for the audience to see it as a neutral word. Even if John Russell Brown is right, then, in pointing out that here are only two overtly anti-Semitic uses of the word in the play, t will surely be seen that overt anti-Semitism very early becomes unnecessary. Each time that *Jew* is used by any of Shylock's enemies, there is a deeply anti-Jewish implication already and automatically assumed.

In Act I, scene iii, after the bond has been struck, Antonio turns to he departing Shylock and murmurs, 'Hie thee gentle Jew./The Hebrew will turn Christian, he grows kind' (173–4). The lines hemselves seem inoffensive, but let us examine the words and the gestures they imply. Shylock has left the stage and Antonio is commenting on the bond that has just been sealed. It is impossible to ignore the mocking tone of Antonio's words and the fact that the scorn they express is directed toward Shylock's Jewishness as much as toward Shylock himself. Surely, too, the elevation of one religion over another is accomplished only at the expense of the religion deemed inferior. To imply that Shylock is so improved (however ironically this is meant) that he verges on becoming Christian is an expression of amused superiority to Jews. The relatively mild anti-Semitism implicit in this passage is significant, both because it is so common in the play and because it leads with the inexorable logic of historical truth to the more fierce and destructive kind of anti-Semitism, borne of fear, that surfaces when the object of it gains ascendancy. While Shylock the Jew is still regarded as a nasty but harmless smudge on the landscape, he is grudgingly accorded some human potential by the Christians; once he becomes a threat to their happiness, however, the quality in him which is initially disdained – his Jewishness – becomes the very cynosure of fear and loathing.

In its early stages, for example, the play makes only light-hearted connections between the Jew and the Devil: as the connections are more and more validated by Shylock's behavior, however, they become charged with meaning. When Launcelot, that dismal clown, is caught in the contortions of indecision as he debates with himself the pros and cons of leaving Shylock's service, he gives the association of Jew and Devil clear expression:

Certainly, my conscience will serve me to run from this Jew my

master . . . to be rul'd by my conscience, I should stay with th‹
Jew my master, who (God bless the mark) is a kind of devil; an‹
to run away from the Jew, I should be rul'd by the fiend, wh‹
(saving your reverence) is the devil himself. Certainly the Jew i
the very devil incarnation, and in my conscience, my conscienc‹
is but a kind of hard conscience, to offer to counsel me to sta`
with the Jew. (II, ii, 1–28)

Significant here is the almost obsessive repetition of 'the Jew'. I‹
the immediate context the phrase has a neat dramatic ambiguity; ›
refers explicitly to Shylock, but by avoiding the use of his name ›
also refers more generally to the concept of the Jew. The ambiguit›
of the phrase makes the demonic association applicable to Jew
generally.

That Launcelot's description is anti-Jewish more than simpl›
anti-Shylock is to be seen in the fact that the view of the Jew ›
presents is in accord with the anti-Semitic portrayal of Jews from
the Middle Ages on. Launcelot's image of the Jew as the Devi›
incarnate conforms to a common medieval notion. It is expressed i‹
Chaucer and much early English drama, and it is given powerfu›
theological support by Luther, who warns the Christian world tha›
'next to the devil thou hast no enemy more cruel, more venemou‹
and violent than a true Jew'.[4] That a fool like Launcelot should tak‹
the assertion a step further and see the Jew as the Devil himself i‹
only to be expected. And that the play should show, as its fina›
discovery, that Shylock is only a devil *manque* is merely to len‹
further support to Luther's influential asseveration.

A less mythological but more colourful and dramatically effectiv‹
anti-Jewish association is forged by the frequent and almos›
casually employed metaphor of Jew as dog. The play is replete wit›
dialogue describing Shylock in these terms. In the mouth o›
Solanio, for example, the connection is explicit: 'I never heard ‹
passion so confus'd,/So strange, outrageous, and so variable/A‹
the dog Jew did utter in the streets' (II, viii, 12–14). I do not believe
that it is going too far to suggest that in this passage the word
strange carries a host of anti-Semitic reverberations. It recalls to the
traditional anti-Semitic memory the foreign and, to the ignorant,
frightening Jewish rituals of mourning – rituals which in anti-
Semitic literature have been redolent with implications of the
slaughter of Christian children and the drinking of their blood.
With this report of Shylock's rage and grief comes a massive turning

point in the play. The once verminous Jew is implicitly transformed into a fearful force.

To this argument I must relate a point about a passage hardly noticed in the critical literature on the play. Having bemoaned his losses and decided to take his revenge, Shylock turns to Tubal and tells him to get an officer to arrest Antonio. 'I will have the heart of him if he forfeit, for were he out of Venice I can make what merchandise I will. Go, Tubal,' he says, 'and meet me at our synagogue, – go good Tubal, – at our synagogue, Tubal' (III, i, 119–20). This collusive and sinister request to meet at the synagogue has always seemed to me to be the most deeply anti-Semitic remark in the play. It is ugly and pernicious precisely because it is indirect. What is the word synagogue supposed to mean in the context? Shylock has just determined to cut the heart out of the finest man in Venice; worse yet, the knowledge that he is legally entitled to do so brings him solace in his grief. Now what might an Elizabethan have thought the synagogue really was? Is it possible that he thought it merely a place where Jews prayed? Is it not more likely that he thought it a mysterious place where strange and terrible rituals were enacted? Whatever Shakespeare himself might have thought, the lines convey the notion that Shylock is repairing to his place of worship immediately after learning that he can now legally murder the good Antonio. Bloodletting and religious worship are brought into a very ugly and insidious conjunction.

Slightly earlier Tubal is observed approaching. Solanio remarks, 'Here comes another of the tribe, – a third cannot be match'd, unless the devil himself turn Jew' (III, i, 70–1). Incredible as it may seem, this line has been used to demonstrate that the play is not anti-Semitic, because Shylock and Tubal alone among the Jews are so bad as to be like devils. What the lines more probably mean is that these two villains are the worst Jews around, and that as the worst of a very bad lot they must be pretty bad.

In her study of the origins of modern German anti-Semitism Lucy Dawidowicz discerns two irreconcilable images of Jews in anti-Semitic literature,

. . . both inherited from the recent and medieval treasury of anti-Semitism. One was the image of the Jew as vermin, to be rubbed out by the heel of the boot, to be exterminated. The other was the image of the Jew as the mythic omnipotent super-adversary, against whom war on the greatest scale had to be conducted. The Jew was, on the one hand, a germ, a bacillus, to be killed without conscience. On the other hand, he was, in the phrase Hitler repeatedly used . . . the 'mortal enemy' (*Todfiend*) to be killed in self-defense.[5]

The Christians in *The Merchant of Venice* initially see Shylock in terms of the first image. He is a dog to be spurned and spat upon. His Jewish gaberdine and his Jewish habits of usury mark him as a cur to be kicked and abused. (Is it likely that Antonio would enjoy the same license to kick a rich Christian moneylender with impunity?) As Shylock gains in power, however, the image of him as a cur changes to an image of him as a potent diabolical force. In Antonio's eyes Shylock's lust for blood takes on the motive energy of Satanic evil, impervious to reason or humanity.

> I pray you think you question with the Jew, –
> You may as well go stand upon the beach
> And bid the main flood bate his usual height,
> You may as well use question with the wolf,
> Why he hath made the ewe bleak for the lamb:
> You may as well forbid the mountain pines
> To wag their high tops, and to make no noise
> When they are fretten with the gusts of heaven:
> You may as well do any thing most hard
> As seek to soften that – than which what's harder? –
> His Jewish heart!

> (IV, i, 70–80)

In this speech Shylock, is utterly 'the Jew' – the embodiment of his species. And the Jew's Jewish heart is wholly obdurate. He is a force of evil as strong as nature itself. No longer a dog to be controlled by beating and kicking, he has become an untamable wolf, an inferno of evil and hatred. The logical conclusion of sentiments like these, surely, is that the Jew must be kept down. Once he is up, his instinct is to kill and ravage. Indeed, Shylock has said as much himself: 'Thou call'dst me dog before thou hadst a cause,/But since I am a dog, beware my fangs' (III, iii, 6–7). If the play defines Christianity as synonymous with tolerance and kindness and forgiveness, it defines Jewishness in opposite terms. The symbol of evil in

The Merchant of Venice is Jewishness, and Jewishness is represented by the Jew.

The counterargument to the charge that Shakespeare is guilty of anti-Semitism has always depended upon the demonstration that the portrait of Shylock is, ultimately, a deeply humane one – that Shylock's arguments against the Christians are unassailable and that his position in the Christian world has resulted from that world's treatment of him. This view, romantic in inception, still persists in the minds of a large number of critics and directors. From such authors as John Palmer and Harold Goddard one gets the image of a Shylock who carries with him the Jewish heritage of suffering and persecution, Shylock as bearer of the pain of the ages. This Shylock is religious and dignified, wronged by the world he inhabits, a man of whom the Jewish people can justly be proud and in whose vengeful intentions they may recognize a poetic righting of the wrongs of Jewish history.[6] That Jews have themselves recognized such a Shylock in Shakespeare's play is borne out in the self-conscious effusions of Heinrich Heine, for whom the Jewish moneylender possessed 'a breast that held in it all the martyrdom . . . [of] a whole tortured people'.[7]

The usual alternative to this view is that of the critics who see Shylock as no more than a stereotyped villain. For these critics, what his sympathizers regard as Shakespeare's plea for Shylock's essential humanity (the 'Hath not a Jew eyes' speech [III, i, 52 ff.]) is nothing more than a justification for revenge. These critics circumvent the charge that Shakespeare is anti-Semitic by arguing that Shylock is not so much a Jew as a carryover from the old morality plays. Albert Wertheim, for example, asserts that 'Shylock is a stylized and conventional comic villain and no more meant to be a realistic portrayal of a Jew than Shakespeare's Aaron is meant to be a realistic Moor.[8] John P. Sisk confidently declares that 'Kittredge was mainly right in his contention that the play is not an anti-Semitic document.'[9] These views are determindly anti-sentimental and usefully balance the oversensitive opposing position. Their mainstay is dramatic precedent, from which can be deduced the similarities between Shylock and the stereotypical comic villain of earlier dramatic modes. Toby Lelyveld notes striking resemblances between Shylock and the Pantalone figure of *commedia dell'arte*, for example: 'In physical appearance, mannerisms and the situations in which he is placed, Shylock is so like his

Italian prototype that his characterization, at least superficially, presents no new aspects save that of its Jewishness.'[10]

What the two critical opinions have in common is their determination to defend Shakespeare from the charge of anti-Semitism – but from opposite sides of the fence. Shylock is either a better man than we might be disposed to believe or he is not really human.[11] The latter reading seems to me to be closer to what the play presents. It is undoubtedly true that Shylock's 'humanity' has frequently been given full – even excessive – play in the theatre. But it is always useful to bear in mind that he is the play's villain. All his words, even the most convincingly aggrieved among them, are the words of a cold, heartless killer and should therefore be regarded skeptically. Shylock is untouched by the plight of those around him, and he plots the ruthless murder of Antonio. Pity for him therefore strikes me as grossly misplaced, and the view of him as the embodiment of wickedness seems dramatically correct. His argument that he is like other men and that he is vengeful only because he has been wronged by them is a violent corruption of the true state of things. Shylock is cruel and monstrous and utterly unlike other men in their capacity for love, fellowship, and sympathy. Consider his remark that he would not have exchanged the ring his daughter stole for a wilderness of monkeys. Rather than redeeming him, as Kirschbaum points out, it only makes him the worse; by demonstrating that he is capable of sentiment and aware of love, it 'blackens by contrast his inhumanity all the more'.[12] As a sincerely expressed emotion the line is out of character. It is the only reference to his wife in the play, and, if we are to take his treatment of Jessica as an indication of his treatment of those he professes to hold dear, we may reasonably conclude that it is a heartfelt expression not of love but of sentimental self-pity. Shylock is, in short, a complete and unredeemed villain whose wickedness is a primary trait. It is a trait, moreover, that is reinforced by the fact of his Jewishness, which, to make the wickedness so much the worse, is presented as synonymous with it.

And yet, although Shylock is the villain of the play, the critics who have been made uneasy by the characterization of his evil have sensed a dimension of pathos, a quality of humanity, that is part of the play. Audiences and readers have usually found themselves pitying Shylock in the end, even though the play's other characters, having demolished him, hardly give the wicked Jew a second thought. The Christians fail to see the humanity of Shylock, not because they are less sensitive than readers and spectators, but because that humanity emerges only in the end, during the court scene when they are understandably caught up in the atmosphere of happiness that surrounds Antonio's release from death. Audiences and readers, whose attention is likely to be equally shared by Antonio and Shylock, are more aware of what is happening to Shylock. They are therefore aware of the change that is forced upon him. To them he is more than simply an undone villain. He is a suffering human being.

Shylock becomes a pitiable character only during his last appearance in the court of Venice. It is here that he is humanized – during a scene in which he is usually silent. Ironically, it is not in his pleadings or self-justifications that Shylock becomes a sympathetic figure, but in his still and silent transformation from a crowing blood-hungry monster into a quiescent victim whose fate lies in the hands of those he had attempted to destroy. How this transmogrification is accomplished is, perhaps, best explained by Gordon Craig's exquisitely simple observation about the chief character of *The Bells*. Craig remarked that 'no matter who the human being may be, and what his crime, the sorrow which he suffers must appeal to our hearts . . .'[13] This observation helps explain why the scene of reversal which turns aside the impending catastrophe of *The Merchant of Venice* does not leave the audience with feelings of unmixed delight in the way that the reversals of more conventional comedies do. The reversal of *The Merchant of Venice* defies a basic premise of the normal moral logic of drama. Instead of merely enjoying the overthrow of an unmitigated villain, we find ourselves pitying him. The conclusion of the play is thus a triumph of ambiguity: Shakespeare has sustained the moral argument which dictates Shylock's undoing while simultaneously compelling us to react on an emotional level more compassionate than intellectual.

If it is true that Jewishness in the play is equated with wickedness, it is surely unlikely that Shylock's elaborate rationalizations of his behaviour are intended to render him as sympathetic. Embedded in the lengthy speeches of self-justification are statements of fact that ring truer to Shylock's motives than the passages in which he identifies himself as wrongly and malevolently persecuted. In his first encounter with Antonio, for example, Shylock explains in a deeply felt aside why he hates the Christian merchant: I hate him for he is a Christian:/But more, for that in low simplicity/He lends out money gratis, and brings down/The rate of

usance here with us in Venice' (I, iii, 37–40). It is only as an
afterthought that he ponders the larger question of Antonio's
hatred of the Jews. The chief reason Shylock gives for hating
Antonio – and he announces it as the chief reason – is directly
related to his avarice in money matters.

Almost all of Shylock's speeches can convincingly be interpreted
in this light. When he speaks, Shylock is a sarcastic character both
in the literal sense of flesh-rending and in the modern sense of
sneering. For example, when he describes the bloody agreement as
a 'merry bond', the word *merry* becomes charged with a sinister
ambiguity. Until the scene of his undoing, Shylock's character is
dominated by the traits usual to Elizabethan comic villains. He is a
hellish creature, a discontented soul whose vilifying of others
marks him as the embodiment of malevolence and misanthropy.
After Jessica's escape Shylock is seen vituperating his daughter, not
mourning her, bemoaning the loss of his money as much as the loss
of his child. His affirmations of his common humanity with the
Christians, particularly in the 'Hath not a Jew eyes' speech, are
above all meant to justify his thirst for revenge. His allegations that
Antonio has disgraced him, laughed at him, and scorned his nation
only because he is a Jew are lopsided. He is abused chiefly because
he is a devil. The fact of his Jewishness only offers his abusers an
explanation for his diabolical nature; it does not offer them the
pretext to torment an innocent man. His speech of wheedling
self-exculpation is surely intended to be regarded in the way that
beleaguered tenants today might regard the whine of their wealthy
landlord: 'Hath not a landlord eyes? Hath not a landlord organs,
dimensions, senses, affections, passions?' Instead of eliciting
sympathy for an underdog, Shakespeare intended the speech to
elicit detestation for one in a privileged and powerful position who
knowingly and deliberately abases himself in a plea for unmerited
sympathy.

Furthermore, in answer to the tradition which defends Shylock
on the grounds that Shakespeare gave him a sympathetic, self-
protecting speech, we need to be reminded that the assertions it
contains are dependent upon a demonstrable falsehood. The climax
of Shylock's speech, its cutting edge, is his confident cry that his
revenge is justified by Christian precedent: 'If a Jew wrong a Christian, what is his humility? Revenge! If a Christian wrong a Jew,
what should his sufference be by Christian example? – why
revenge!' (III, i, 62–4). In fact what happens is that in return for the

crime which Shylock commits against Antonio, he is offered not revenge but mercy – harshly given perhaps, but mercy nonetheless – and this in circumstances where revenge would be morally and legally sanctioned. The director who causes this speech to be uttered as a genuine defense of its speaker is thus ignoring one of the play's most tangible morals.

Until the court scene, Shylock remains a readily understood and easily identified villain. His dominant characteristics are the negative qualities normally associated with vice figures. Sympathy for him before the reversal therefore does violence to the dramatic purpose of the play. Completely in the ascendancy, he has power and the law itself on his side. When sympathy finally becomes right and proper, it transcends the narrow bounds of religion and stereotype. When finally we are made to pity Shylock, we do not pity a wrongfully persecuted member of an oppressed minority. Instead we pity a justly condemned and justly punished villain. A potential murderer has been caught, is brought to justice, and is duly and appropriately sentenced. The pity we are moved to feel is as natural and inevitable as the great loathing we were made to feel formerly. It results simply from the sympathy that we are likely to admit at any sight of human suffering, no matter how well deserved it may be.

In the court scene the presence of Portia stands as a direct assurance that Antonio will not die. While we remain conscious of Shylock's evil intentions, then, our judgement of him is tempered by our privileged awareness of his ultimate impotence. In other words, although we might despise Shylock, we do not fear him. This distinction is critical to an understanding of his character and of Shakespeare's intentions, and it helps explain the readiness with which we are able to extend sympathy to the villain.

The chief explanation, however, goes somewhat deeper. It is simultaneously psychological and dramatic. It is psychological to the extent that we are willy-nilly affected by the sight of Shylock in pain. It is dramatic to the extent that the scene is so arranged as to dramatize in the subtlest possible way the manifestation of that pain. Shylock remains onstage while his erstwhile victims are restored to prosperity by Portia. The publication of Antonio's rescue and of Shylock's punishment takes ninety-six lines, from Portia's 'Tarry a little, there is something else . . .' (IV, i, 301) to Gratiano's gleeful 'Had I been judge, thou shouldst have had ten more,/To bring thee to the gallows, not to the font' (ll, 395–6).

During this period – about five minutes – Shylock is transformed from a villain into a victim.

In part the inversion is achieved by use of the established fool, Gratiano, who, by trumpeting the victory of the Christians, assumes Shylock's earlier role as one who enjoys another's pain. Gratiano is a character who talks too much, who suspects silence, who prefers to play the fool. His joy in Shylock's downfall becomes sadistic and self-serving. Interestingly, it is not shared in quite so voluble a fashion by the other Christian characters. Portia has done all the work, and yet it is Gratiano – whose real contribution to the scene is to announce Portia's success and to excoriate the Jew – who cries at Shylock 'Now, infidel, I have you on the hip' (l. 334). Until this point in the play Shylock has been vicious and sadistic, nastily rubbing his hands in anticipation of a bloody revenge, thriving on the smell of the blood he is about to taste. Now that role is taken from him by Gratiano, on whom it sits unattractively. The failure of his friends to partipate in this orgy of revenge suggests that their feelings are more those of relief at Antonio's release than of lust for Shylock's blood.

As the tables are turned upon him, Shylock gradually and unexpectedly reveals a new dimension of himself, and the farcical pleasure we have been led to expect is subverted by his surprising response to defeat. He reveals a capacity for pain and suffering. As a would-be murderer, Shylock gets at least what he deserves. As a human being asking for mercy, he receives, and possibly merits, sympathy. Shylock recognizes instantly that he has been undone. Once Portia reminds him that the bond does not allow him to shed one drop of blood, his orgy is over and he says little during the scene of dénouement. 'Is that the law?' he lamely asks. Five lines later, he is ready to take his money and leave the court with whatever remaining dignity is permitted him. But an easy egress is not to be his. He is made to face the consequences of his evil. Portia's addresses to Shylock during the confrontation are disguised exhortations to him to suffer for the wrong he has done. She forces him to acknowledge her triumph and his defeat: 'Tarry a little' (l. 301); 'Soft . . . soft, no haste!' (ll. 316–7); 'Why doth the Jew pause?' (l. 331); 'Therefore prepare thee to cut' (l. 320); 'Tarry Jew' (l. 343); 'Art thou contented Jew? What dost thou say?' (l. 388). Shylock is made to stand silently, receiving and accepting mercy and some restitution from Antonio; he is compelled to bear, not the stings of revenge upon himself, but the sharper stings of a forgiveness that he is incapable of giving. His humiliation lies in his inability to refuse the gift of life from one whose life he maliciously sought. When he requests leave to go from the court, the change that has come over him is total. He is no longer a figure of vice, and he has not become a figure of fun (except, perhaps, to Gratiano). He is a lonely, deprived, and defeated creature feeling pain. The fact that he has caused his own downfall does not diminish the sympathy felt for him now, in part because of the protraction of his undoing, and in part because of the dramatic effect of the change in him. The suddenness of the alteration of his character forces a comparison between what he once was and what he has become. And where dramatic energy is its own virtue, the visible eradication of that energy is a source of pathos.

In this scene the word *Jew* has been used like a blunt instrument by Portia and Gratiano. Now, being used against one who has become a victim, the former associations of the word are thrown into question. Portia's persistence in doing to the Jew as he would have done to Antonio has a strangely bitter effect. She hunts him when he is down; she throws the law in his teeth with a righteousness that seems repulsive to us primarily because we have long been aware that Antonio was ultimately invulnerable. Having removed Shylock's sting, she is determined to break his wings in the bargain. In this determination, she is unlike her somewhat dull but more humane husband, who is prepared to pay Shylock the money owed him and to allow him to leave. Portia's stance is beyond legal questioning, of course. What gives us pause is the doggedness with which she exacts justice. Shylock is ruined by adversity and leaves the stage without even the strength to curse his foes: 'I pray you give me leave to go from hence,/I am not well' (ll. 391–2). He communicates his pain by his powerlessness, and the recognition of this pain stirs the audience.

In a brief space, in which his silence replaces his usual verbosity, Shylock is transformed. A villain is shown to be more than merely villainous. Shylock is shown to be more than merely the Jew. He is shown to possess a normal, unheroic desire to live at any cost. The scene of undoing is an ironic realization of Shylock's previously histrionic pleas for understanding. We now see something that formerly there was no reason to believe: that if you prick him, Shylock bleeds.

By endowing Shylock with humanity in the end Shakespeare would seem to have contradicted the dominating impression of the play, in which the fierce diabolism of the Jew is affirmed in so many ways. And indeed, the contradiction is there. Having described a character who is defined by an almost otherwordly evil, whose life is one unremitting quest for an unjust vengeance, it seems inconsistent to allow that he is capable of normal human feelings. The Jew has been used to instruct the audience and the play's Christians about the potential and essential evil of his race; he has been used to show that a Jew with power is a terrible thing to behold, is capable of the vilest sort of destruction. And the play has demonstrated in the person of his daughter that the only good Jew is a Christian. The contradiction emerges almost in spite of Shakespeare's anti-Semitic design. He has shown on the one hand, by the creation of a powerful and dominant dramatic image, that the Jew is inhuman. But he seems to have been compelled on the other hand to acknowledge that the Jew is also a human being.

The most troubling aspect of the contradictory element of *The Merchant of Venice* is this: if Shakespeare knew that Jews were human beings like other people – and the conclusion of the play suggests that he did – and if he knew that they were not *merely* carriers of evil but human creatures with human strengths and weaknesses, then the play as a whole is a betrayal of the truth. To have used it as a means for eliciting feelings of loathing for Jews, while simultaneously recognizing that its portrayal of the race it vilifies is inaccurate or, possibly, not the whole truth, is profoundly troubling. It is as though *The Merchant of Venice* is an anti-Semitic play written by an author who is not an anti-Semite – but an author who has been willing to use the cruel stereotypes of that ideology for mercenary and artistic purposes.

8 The History of *King Lear*

It is a curious fact that *King Lear*, a play which depends as no other upon a decisive event preceding the beginning of the first scene, presents its pre-play past in a vague, usually shadowy light through the use of allusion and a kind of spontaneous reference[1] only ephemerally and fragmentarily realized. On this score criticism is fairly unanimous. While it is recognized that a kind of abstract primitivism powerfully asserts itself in the play,[2] and that the language reverberates with biblical allusions, it is simultaneously noted that, for example, the play 'does not invite us to speculate about antecedent actions',[3] and that Lear 'alone of all the tragic heroes, never interests as a husband or a lover'[4] because he seems to have no existence as either in the tragedy. Indeed, the drama as a whole offers very little of lives formerly lived. Yet the hints of those lives are there and earlier existence is given fleeting attention, its relevance to the present occasionally, if briefly, illuminated. In its use of the past, *King Lear* makes a striking contrast with a play like *Othello*, whose hero derives his notions of self from conscious and extensive recollections of that world and his locus in it, or with such a play as *Antony and Cleopatra* whose past has been characterized by Robert Ornstein as 'Vaster than orgiastic memory [touching] every character and every scene . . .'[5]. In these two plays the past provides continuity, but in *King Lear* there is instead what John Reibetanz calls a 'sequential discontinuity', which results from the absence of a clear sense of what existed before the play.[6]

In *King Lear* I count some twenty-four allusions and direct references to the characters' physical existence before the events of the play. Of these twenty-four references only a handful seem to be crucial to an understanding of the present – the play itself: these moments tend to provide the characters of the play – chiefly Lear – with the usually missing element of a past life by anchoring them in a real, if almost imperceptible personal and political history. Notwithstanding Wilson Knight's warning that 'it is dangerous to

119

abstract the personal history of the protagonist from his environment',[7] the absence of such a history in this play makes the matter demand investigation. As Lear's tragedy becomes more manifest with the progression of the plot, the past becomes more defined, the allusions somewhat more sure and precise, and the characters more confident and self-knowing. Of the references to the pre-play past in *King Lear*, fourteen belong to Lear, three to Kent, one to Cordelia, one each to Goneril and Regan, one to Edgar, one to the First Servant, one to the Old Man, and one to Gloucester (see Appendix).

Indeed the drama opens upon a discussion between Gloucester and Kent about their past common misapprehension of the king's affections. As the play begins, each of them is confessing his own need to correct a false past impression. But, like many of the allusions to the past in the first scene, theirs are indirect, unspecific and general. Gloucester is careful to balance the past error against the contradiction of the present discovery:

> Kent.   I thought the King had more affected the Duke
>   of Albany than Cornwall.
> Glou.   It did always seem so to us; but now, in the
>   division of the kingdom, it appears not which of
>   the Dukes he values most.   (I, 1, 1–5)

In this kind of general allusion to the way in which the past has been apprehended and the next more specific memory of Edmund's conception – 'there was good sport at his making' (I, i, 23) – are indicated the two kinds of history upon which the past is founded. History is the thing done and the thing remembered, the political and personal past at strange odds in the minds of the characters of the drama. Strength and confidence seem to be shored up by the exactly remembered act, while mere assumptions about earlier life challenge the conceptions of self in the present.

For all character analysis must start with the question of who the character is. The answer, itself ideologically fraught, depends upon the critical assumption that a 'self' can be known in a text, that a character's words and actions define his means of connecting to his world in a complex coalescence of time, space, and ideology. The contradiction identified above is illustrative of this concatenation of forces and suggestive of the whimsical nature of historical knowledge. Kent and Gloucester are agreed that they thought one thing and that present evidence shows them to have been wrong. That is, their former assumptions related them to a political situation in a false way. They are there discussing their world in a large social sense. However, when Gloucester can recall Edmund's 'making' he is harking back to absolutely known private and indisputable memory; a part of history, that is, which is his to control and remember without fear of contradiction. Hence, whatever the distaste so long and widely expressed about this public and humiliating comment in Edmund's presence, its significance really lies in its reflection of Gloucester's use of it to link himself to a past world which is his alone. It is a means of reasserting his certainty of his past, of reestablishing the known self which has been confused by the king's unpredictable act.

Lear's 'Meantime' (I, i, 36) signifies a desire and an attempt to balance past and present in a way that gathers powerful meaning through the rest of the scene. The word is defined in the *OED* as 'During or within the time which intervenes between one specified period or event and another' and takes dramatic shape from the events which immediately follow. His words, which concentrate upon present apprehensions of future life – ''tis our fast intent' (I, i, 38) – are hugely contingent upon the surely and completely known past action – 'Know that we have divided/In three our kingdom'; (I, i, 37–8) – and unwittingly comprehend the modes of response to his test provided by Goneril and Regan and Cordelia. In the speeches of Goneril and Regan emphasis is placed surely in the present tense. Their styles are impersonal, general, and asseverative of present love. The bases of their professed love are absent because, naturally, their 'love' has no bases; it relates to no known or shared past affection. Rich and lovely though the speeches are, they are anchorless and might as easily, with only slight modification, be addressed to any lover. Each, in essence, asserts, 'I love you', but eschews the very essential to which Cordelia compulsively and necessarily returns – that is, the past love, the function of love, the common life which has brought father and daughter towards this present love. In writing about Lear's rejection of Cordelia's 'bond', Lawrence Danson makes the point that the bond itself is 'expressive of traditional values, shared beliefs, of history itself', and that the 'old way', as Danson calls this shared past, has been radically dislocated.[8]

So, when Cordelia speaks, at last, it behoves her to reach back-

ward in time as a way of dividing herself from her sisters and of
bringing into focus the relationship between herself and the king –
the father and daughter with a shared past. It is noteworthy that in
Goneril's and Regan's speeches the only references to Lear himself
are the impersonal 'Sir' and the generalized 'father' in, 'as much as
child e'er lov'd, or father found', (Goneril, 54–9) and 'your dear
highness' (Regan, 75). Cordelia, on the other hand strikes directly
at the personal, precise details of the past lives of herself and the
king; 'You have begot me, bred me, lov'd me: I/Return those duties
back as are right fit,/Obey you, love you, and most honour you'
(96–8). The thoughts are balanced not merely by the symmetry of
the syllables in the first and third lines quoted but, additionally, by
the logical conjunction of the two temporal spheres which place
past and present into a sequential order: past begetting has brought
present obedience, past breeding present love, past love present
honour. There is a completeness accessible in Cordelia's confident
couplings which bespeaks the fulfilment of love's obligation and
feelings. The confidence seems to derive from the consciously
remembered past, a past which is here publically presented in
terms of a shared experience and founded upon the nearly tangible
relationship between the father and daughter. The precision of
Cordelia's response derives in part from the way in which she
assumes a linkage between herself and Lear in her memory of what
binds them and is emphasized by the biting consonants of *begot*,
bred, and, even, *lov'd*.

    Lear's response to Cordelia vacillates between heroic abuse and
passionate self-pity, modes which, because they are so violently
yoked, suggest the spontaneous urge for balance within the
speaker's mind. We may consider, for example, the vast intellectual
and emotional space between such immense monstrosity as

> The barbarous Scythian,
> Or he that makes his generation messes
> To gorge his appetite, shall to my bosom
> Be as well neighbour'd, piti'd, and reliev'd,
> As thou my sometimes daughter,

                                              (116–19)

and the later purely felt, but comparatively imprecise, 'I lov'd her
most, and thought to set my rest/On her kind nursery' (122–3). This

last expression, so utter in sheer misery, is a spontaneous yet vague return to that shared experience with his favourite daughter which Lear seems to know only through the agency of feeling. In the play it is this very feeling of love which keeps rising to the surface of his mind, and keeps expressing itself against his will in the tormented but somehow shapeless thoughts which he forces himself to suppress.

Kent's intervention provides the antidote of specificity to the fuming chaos of the king's ire. He speaks with the force of confident knowledge of himself and the king. His speech includes details of love which offer a direct perspective on the past perception of Lear and himself. He has known Lear as king, father, master and patron:

> Royal Lear,
> Whom I have ever honour'd as my King,
> Lov'd as my father, as my master follow'd,
> As my great patron thought on in my prayers, –

> (140–2)

He has willingly risked his life in battle for Lear:

> My life I never held but as a pawn
> To wage against thine enemies.

> (155–6)

Thus, as Kent and Cordelia brave the present calamity, they derive their strength to do so from their certainties about their own *loci* in the past that have made this present real. Their comprehension of the sheer wrong of what is occurring is given moral authority by their perception of the crisis as a continuation of personal history. Each of them notes a relationship to Lear that is direct, immediate, and personal: Cordelia, almost informally, sees herself bound to her father by the near equation of 'You' and 'I'; Kent's acknowledgement of his loyal subservience to Lear is manifested in his reference to 'my King', 'my father', 'my master'. By contrast, in the love professions of Goneril and Regan, Lear is 'Sir' – in the Quarto both commence their speeches with 'Sir' – he is the rather abstract 'father' in Goneril's, 'As much as child e'er lov'd, or father found', (58) and he is 'your dear highness' (76). Their speeches tend by this

formality and generalization to separate them from the object of
their professed love, while those of Kent and Cordelia move in the
opposite direction by the tendency to personalize by linking
speaker and object in a vital relationship. The vitality owes everything to the presence in the speeches of that pre-play past by which
the bonds are given concrete and ineradicable form.

Alone together at the end of this scene, Goneril and Regan take
the opportunity to discuss their version of history in relation to the
present; to make of the pre-play past a justificatory myth by which
the future can be twisted into serving themselves. Like most of
Shakespeare's villains, the sisters demonstrate only a fragmented
connection with history. Their mode, typically, is the present and
future, their vision is clearly focussed on gaining control of their
world by looking at what is, rather than what was, in order to
determine what shall be. Goneril knows in common with everyone
in the court that Lear 'always lov'd our sister most', (290) Regan that
'he hath ever but slenderly known himself' (293–394). These two
'facts' about the past are expressed not as evidence of their knowledge of or shared experience with the king but, on the contrary, as
demonstrations of his vulnerability to them. They see in the present
not the maniacal inconsistency which Kent and Cordelia perceive
in his present behaviour, but a further example of how he is to be
wholly discomfited and, more interestingly, *why* he is to be subjected to their wills. His 'unconstant starts' (300) infirmities of age,
and 'changes' (288) give them what we might least expect them to
need – a moral basis for their hitting together against their father's
'unruly waywardness' (298). Their last words in the scene demonstrate their mode of apprehending time forcefully and significantly:

> Reg.   We shall further think of it.
> Gon.   We must do something, and i'th' heat.

>   (307–8)

That is, what is now is merely a means to future control.

The past that haunts and tortures Lear is the event of the first
scene. It is this that threatens his present and future, this that
unbalances the equipoise he strove for in his careful but ultimately
disastrous attempt to determine history – to prevent future strife.
The madness he fears, while it stems from his banishment of
Cordelia, has deep roots in that vaguely but profoundly felt lifetime

of knowledge of Cordelia. His present pain threatens to destroy him because he is as yet incapable of seeking beyond the act which has led to it; he cannot acknowledge the violence he has done to a history of love. The banishment of Cordelia and its consequences compel Lear to live on the very edge of the present. His life, from the interrupted sojourn with Goneril until the death of Cordelia is a series of dangerous augmenting crises, each of which has to be faced on the available present terms. The simple *time* does not allow reflection, and the circumstances, with their rapid plunge from one adversity to the next, make the present the overwhelmingly relevant sphere. That pre-play past is in evidence, but to Lear its connection with the situations he faces is ephemeral and spontaneous. Sometimes it rises to his thoughts almost unconsciously and seems at such moments to be oddly disconnected from the present. When for example, he instructs Regan on her filial obligation –

> I know what reason
> I have to think so: if thou shouldst not be glad,
> I would divorce me from thy mother's tomb,
> Sepulchring an adult'ress.

> (II, iv, 130–4)

– his dead wife, her dead mother, the common bond between them, is merely the instrument of debate. Indeed, the detail has been winnowed from that amorphous experience of both father and daughter here, but it is twisted into the grotesque shape of distorted conception – a metaphorical point in an argumentative assertion which becomes little more than a meaningless threat.

It is not until much later that Lear is seen looking farther back than the beginning of the action, beyond his own immediate plight and its immediate cause. It is only minutes before the encounter with Poor Tom that he acknowledges that past in a single passionate exclamation which brings with powerful certainty a reminder of that life and its imperatives: 'O! I have ta'en/Too little care of this' (III, iv, 32–3). As the previous allusion to the past was conditional and separated Lear from the past by bringing the allusion into the present – 'I would divorce me' – this present reference propels the king back into the past, consciously making him and it inseparable. The sentence is a recognition of a specific locus in history. It acknowledges power, authority, and humanity in a way that has not been evident in Lear's self-expression until now. In this sense the memory stands apart from the speech even though it serves as a foundation for the ideological generalization which is built upon it. And it is significant that Lear's first such recognition has reference to himself not as the father of the wronged maid but as the thing he most is in the drama, the king of his nation. The recognition, then, possesses great clarity in its identification of a self directly connected with national history. It relates to the opening lines of the play in its acknowledgement of past error, and it indicates, like that opening, the possibility of change, of a reassessment of the present. Thus, by a linking of the personal to the political pasts, an old assumption, a past 'truth', is subjected to radical revision which, in turn, makes necessary a radical reconsideration of the formerly stable self.

Through the terrible miasma of his madness details of that life leap into sudden focus, informing the lexis of insanity with a precise relationship to that old fragmenting self. 'Tray, Blanch, and Sweetheart' (III, vi, 64) so affectionately named, link the king here to that other part of his early self, the domestic paternal persona, betrayed, even here, by his own bitches – 'see, they bark at me' (64). In those moments, when the past acquires clarity for Lear, there is a recognizable consistency: for as the present is fraught with a paranoic certainty of the adversity of all forces, human and natural, so does old experience take the forms of aggressive challenge. The slowly growing knowledge of himself as a traitor to himself and his kingdom is lent authority by such lucid yet disconnected flashes from personal and political history.

Between the memory of his dogs and his next, much later, memory of his old world are two recollections of that world by two nameless characters who, not unlike Cordelia, discover in that old world and their memory of it, reasons for doing good through self sacrifice. Two men find reasons in their pasts for their present courageous defiance of authority. Cornwall's servant, enraged by his master's cruelty – 'take the chance of anger' (III, vi, 78) – kills him as he is killed by Goneril. His power to act against his master and his habit of loyalty derive from an older and more demanding loyalty to a code of righteous wrath from which he draws present strength:

Hold your hand, my Lord.

> I have serv'd you ever since I was a child,
> But better service have I never done you
> Than now to bid you hold.

> (71–4)

And, in similar fashion, the old Man risks 'hurt' to lead the blind Gloucester to Edgar out of loyalty to an old code of loyalty which present times are destroying.

> O my good Lord!
> I have been your tenant, and your father's tenant,
> These fourscore years,

> (IV, i, 12–4)

In these two quickly passed moments, when the values of old times are seen asserting themselves so vividly and dramatically, we discover one of the deepest consistencies of the play. In each case defiance of authority is motivated by a code which is personalized through history. But the fragility of the old ideologies is demonstrated in the death of the servant and the feebleness of the old man. Yet, though imperiled, these ideologies, because so related to old experience and memory of the past, are ultimately as irrepressible as human nature.

In stubborn contrast to the lucidity of the two anonymous servants, Lear's madness in Act IV, scene vi reflects dreadful temporal confusion by the nature of the old memories and the ways in which they assert their presence in the introrsed mind of the king as it seems to burst apart by virtue of the forces which thrust and twist against each other. The past is understood as a concrete structure of certain facts as when he declares that 'Gloucester's bastard son/Was kinder to his father than my daughters/Got 'tween the lawful sheets' (117–9). No detail emerges in the assertion, no recollection of the 'sport' in their making. And yet the implication of memory is overpowering simply by virtue of the assumptions of the allusion. It must nevertheless be linked to the earlier questioning of Regan's legitimacy which the present allusion categorically and automatically rejects. This moment merely uses the past as a kind of rhetorical basis for the present declaration.

However, in the encounter of Lear and Gloucester two phrases
echo terribly: each of them relating directly to an old knowledge
which binds each old man to the other by the tough cords of the
past. Gloucester, encountering Lear knows him immediately
because he remembers his voice: 'The trick of that voice I do well
remember:/Is't not the King?' (IV, vi, 109–10). His apprehension is,
of course, entirely dependent upon his sense of hearing. The past
brings a tragic kind of comfort to the old man whose bearings are
lost but who is suddenly able to winnow comfort simply from the
sound of a familiar voice. The old detail – the sound of the king's
voice – brings order of a kind to the lost wandering old man. Lear's
more terrible plight is given added force by his mad echo of
Gloucester's recollection; for him there is no possibility of calm as
his own crazy recognition drives him towards further confusion.
Indeed he knows Gloucester ['I know thee well enough; thy name is
Gloucester' (179)], but the manner of knowing him is far from what
his senses inform him. 'I remember thine eyes well enough' (138)
addressed to the eyeless man is spectacularly impossible but
throws into relief the driving dramatic point about the nature of
Lear's delusion; that is, he is betrayed here by his own senses. And
yet, he does know the other old man. His past, then, is a constant
and real element in the amorphous present. When Lear appeals to
Gloucester's sympathy, he does so on the basis of a shared memory
from the past: 'Thou has seen a farmer's dog bark at a beggar?' (156).
An actual detail from common life links the two in a sympathetic
alliance. The bond of that alliance is the fact of their age, the
instinctual or sensuous felt experience which both acknowledge,
and the mutual recognition. When Lear acknowledges Gloucester
by name he appeals to that knowledge on the basis of a commonplace whose significance seems to lie in part in its connection of the
two old men in a shared experience of infancy – as it connects them
to all men. But the fact that it declares the existence of a past in the
tenses of the past cannot be ignored, for it is the presence of that
tense which unites them:

> Thy name is Gloucester;
> Thou must be patient; we came crying hither:
> Thou know'st the first time that we smell the air
> We wawl and cry.

(180–3)

The past is allowed to assert itself in the present scene in the three ways common to the play – it is here by virtue of sensory memory – sound and sight – by virtue of shared experience of ordinary life – the farmer's dog at the gate – and by virtue of the way in which the present experience is explained by reference to the unremembered but known history of life – we wawl when first we smell the air. As Gloucester's memory of Lear's voice brings the vestige of order to his mind when it is forced to connect with the structures of the past, so even Lear, clad in what Cordelia later refers to as the 'weeds' of recent 'memories' (IV, vii, 7) and fretted in mind, nevertheless finds the basis of order in madness in his recollections of life before the commencement of present events. For it is from these bases that arise the great and terrifying generalizations which render his plight as both itself, deeply individually felt, and part of that larger human history which has become so elusive in the present.

But it is in the last moments of the play's last great scene that Lear's past and present merge in a short but concentrated series of wrenching exclamations. Lear, *'with* Cordelia *dead in his arms'*, brings into conjunction those temporal spheres which have wandered in disorder through the play. The pre-play past, the play's past, the present and the future are contained; the detailed and the generalized knowledge of past life tumble to the fore of the king's present consciousness and, in a way that is only apparently random, give a sureness and stability to Lear which has not been evident before now but which, we instinctively feel, was once natural to him. From the terrible yet definitive recognition that 'she's dead as earth' (V, ii, 261) flows the remorseless knowledge of infinity and eternity, of all that has been in his life and all that ever will be. 'She's dead as earth' is a statement of absolute present truth. It is the surest statement Lear makes in the course of the play; a felt and known assertion that encompasses both the object of his passion and the entire world which contains it. Cordelia's 'deadness' is the cause of the death of everything. And yet, of course, on one level, the remark is absurd. Lear is surrounded by evidence of life in the grieving persons who observe this end. Nevertheless, the idea of death of the earth signals the apocalyptic end of all life in a consolatory and sympathetic universe. This present physical finality is extended, in his remaining words, to the dimension of time. Kent, Edgar, and Albany each perceive the moment as the last horror of life, as the coalescence of the future with the present. To them the future has died in the present catastrophe.

And yet, while to these three observers of the scene life appears to have lost meaning, it is left to Lear to discover its value. His words of grief, far from the nihilistic dogma of the three survivors, assert, anomalously, the value of life and existence. He discovers the possibility of redemption and articulates its worth.

> Lear. This feather stirs; she lives! if it be so,
>   It is a chance which does redeem all sorrows
>   That ever I have felt.

> (265–7)

The past – the whole of the past – crowds into the present and gives it a perceptible form. Cordelia's life has a terrible equivalent: the sum total of Lear's agonies, of which many have been contained in the events of the play, are willingly offered as an exchange for Cordelia's life. All of the felt sorrows of a life suddenly have a tangible measureable meaning, are offered as a kind of barter in the way that love was once put on the block. Lear's 'redeem' can be seen to possess a mercantile as well as religious connotation. The amorphousness of the past is distilled into a bitter drop of pure pain and offered like a sacrificial object in exchange for a single consoling breath from the dead. But, of course, the sacrifice is not accepted, Cordelia is dead, and the systematic methods of consolation – words, rituals, historical explanation – are without effect.

The 'ever' of that line leads the king to further recognitions of eternity, recognitions which culminate in the great antithetical but logical swing to the repeated nevers which he utters seconds before his own death. When Lear exclaims a few lines later, 'now she's gone for ever!' (270) the single word 'now' calls him forcibly back into the present from that realm of his past where the sorrows of his life are summoned into a single defining form of a measureable value. It is in his recollection of the quality of Cordelia's voice that Lear asserts a kind of control over his own history. He states a fact which leads to a generalization which becomes in the process a clear truth: 'Her voice was ever soft,/Gentle and low, an excellent thing in woman' (272–3). Cordelia's *presence* is related to personal and general history. As Gloucester found comfort in the sound of his king's voice, so Lear here finds in the memory of Cordelia's voice a way of reconciling the present with what once was. Clarity, in other words, increases for Lear as he begins to situate himself in

relation to his and Cordelia's pasts. In this awareness, tragically late
in coming, he seems to be taking the opposite direction of those
Shakespearean characters, described by Alvin Kernan, who are
'caught in the movement of history, driven by their own passions
and the historical forces at work on them', and who lose sight of the
direction their world is taking.[9] There is, Lear's memory tells him, a
phenomenon of continuity by which individual life makes itself felt
and is made a part of the whirling events of history.

It is this realization that must, surely, account for the otherwise
amazingly irrelevant recollection of his own prowess as a sword-
fighter. In one of the most stunningly naturalistic leaps of his mind,
Lear can, with Cordelia dead in his arms, call up a boast from his
memory:

> Did I not fellow?
> I have seen the day, with my good biting falchion
> I would have made them skip: I am old now,
> And these same crosses spoil me.

> (275–8)

In this rejoinder to the officer, the memory of a recent event recalls
the existence of an old skill whose desuetude[10] is brought home by
modernity and present trouble. The cohesion in this sentence of the
two modes of past time – that of and that preceding the play – in
opposition to the present, give the remaining lines of the play and
minutes of life their dynamic form. Lear's mind finds a resting
point just as it begins to wander over the present. His memory of
his old competent self seems to give him the strength briefly to face
the fact of what is. The boast is like a respite from calamity; it takes
him away from here and now and lends him momentary self assurance through a self-defining recollection that the present and the
past conform.

But it is the present only that remains to be faced, divorced from
the past, tangible, terrible, real. This is the fact which makes necessary the 'second ending' of *King Lear*. In the present there is no life
and no breath. The structures of history and memory while
eternally present are revealed as useless, as structures only because
of illusion, desire, and ideology. The forms which life is supposed
to possess – individually yet consistently assumed in the minds of
each character – are linguistic, even socially functional. Characters

in this play, including Lear, who connect through shared assumptions are connecting, after all, on the basis of words and taught feelings. It is, indeed, to words and the kinds of consolations they habitually are understood to contain that Edgar resorts in the end. By his attempt to define the disaster, even in his awareness of its resistance to definition, he is trying to give form and meaning to what has occurred – that is, to assert some kind of human control over human catastrophe. He is giving a perspective to the tragedy even in his assertion of its incomprehensibility. Edgar is making a conventional bow in the direction of what Sheldon Zitner calls the 'demands of form and decorum in language [which] may lead to untruths with a paradoxy that . . . language as literature . . . declares itself inadequate for the task it has . . . performed'.[11] His words, in obedience to the demands of decorum, give the play wholeness and dramatic form. Yet the words are at appalling odds with the last words of the king. Those last words possess the incomprehension to which Edgar's only tentatively allude; they are formless, almost instinctual, gasps whose echoes linger much longer than the official ending. They buffet against the closure which Edgar's historical perspective attempts to provide, and because of their greater feeling – amorphous, unclear – they rupture utterly the human compulsion for neatness in drama and life which Edgar expresses. Lear's last words are a transcendence of the historical and linguistic dogmas by which characters in this play arrange their own *loci* in relation to the events of the present. He digs deep into the very idea of a systematic universe, into the world of nature itself, beyond history and time, and finds nothing. Why should a dog, a horse, a rat, have life? There is no answer because there is no system; there is no god. The last words of Lear are striving not to answer the question but to demonstrate the sheer frightening and hapless coincidence of all things.

The following are the locations of those references to the pre-play world upon which the argument of this chapter is based.

Lear	Cordelia	Kent	Goneril	Regan	Edgar	Gloucester	Old Man
I, i, 37	I,i,95	I,i,1	I,i,290	I,i,293	III,iv,85	I,i,3	IV,i,11
I,i,122		I,i,140					
I,i,234		I,i,155					
II,iv,130							
III,iv,20							
III,iv,33							
III,vi,63							
IV,vi,118							
IV,vi,138							
IV,vi,156							
IV,vi,180							
V,iii,265							
V,iii,265							
V,iii,273							
V,iii,275							

First Servant
III,vii,70

Notes

1 : INTRODUCTION

1. In the rush to remind the world that Shakespeare wrote for the stage it is sometimes forgotten that the actor is necessarily a critic before he is an actor.
2. *Hamlet,* ed. Harold Jenkins, The Arden Shakespeare (London: Methuen, 1982). I have used Arden editions of all the plays discussed in the following pages.

2 : THE RITES OF VIOLENCE IN *1 HENRY IV*

1. Northrop Frye, *Fools of Time* (University of Toronto Press, 1967) p. 4.
2. In *The Scapegoat,* James Frazer discusses the role and function of that human being upon whom the evils and sorrows of the society are concentrated and through the death of whom the society is released from its suffering. The process of Hotspur's death suggests that he is Hal's and the nation's scapegoat. Frazer remarks the many ceremonies in primitive and ancient societies whereby regeneration and purification were possible only after the killing of a human scapegoat or the death of a god (Macmillan: London, 1913) pp. 227 *passim.*
3. In describing dramatic climax, Fredson Bowers emphasizes the conscious ethical decision of that moment in the drama which determines the inevitability of its outcome. He argues that 'the rising complications of the action culminate in a crucial decision by the protagonist, the nature of which constitutes the turning point of the play and will dictate the . . . catastrophe' ('The Structure of *King Lear''*, *Shakespeare Quarterly*, 31, 1 (1980) 8).
4. Lawrence Danson, *Tragic Alphabet* (New Haven and London: Yale University Press, 1974) p. 21.
5. If the status of Hal as hero is acknowledged, we must recognize that it is owed in large measure to the sheer stage power of the soliloquy. Hal's presumption in addressing us directly has the effect of placing him uppermost: he goes beyond the audible reflection of, say, Falstaff on honour, to the point of taking us into his confidence, promising *us* a happy surprise, and then, here, realizing that promise.
6. Virginia M. Carr, 'Once More into the Henriad: ' "Two-Eyed" View', *Journal of English and Germanic Philology*, LXXVII, 4 (Oct. 1978) 535.
7. Carr's reference to the gradualism of the reintroduction of ceremonies

which integrate their primitive substances is consistent with the prince's so-called 'lysis' conversion, described by Sherman Hawkins as one which 'may include more than one crisis experience separated by periods of steady advance'. ('The Structural Problem of *Henry IV*', *Shakespeare Quarterly*, 31, 3 (Autumn 1982) 296). I am suggesting that Hal's use of ritual in this scene is more significant than a single stage of development or an advance to his next strength: he is demonstrating, by this use of the language of ritual, his own actual control of a situation which by rights belongs to the monarch. King Henry's subjection to this control is signalized by the conviction of his acceptance of the vow.

8. Rene Girard, *Violence and the Sacred* (Baltimore: Johns Hopkins University Press, 1979) p. 37.
9. James L. Calderwood, '*1 Henry IV*: Art's Gilded Lie', *English Literary Renaissance*, 3, 1 (Winter 1973) 137.
10. Maynard Mack, 'The Jacobean Shakespeare', *Jacobean Theatre*, eds John Russell Brown and Bernard Hassis (New York: Capricorn Books, 1967) p. 13.
11. Norman Council, 'Prince Hal: Mirror of Success', *Shakespeare Studies*, VII (1974) 142–3.
12. Harold Jenkins, *The Structural Problem in Shakespeare's Henry the Fourth*, (London: Methuen, 1956) p. 9.
13. George Hibbard, *The Making of Shakespeare's Dramatic Poetry* (University of Toronto Press, 1981) p. 180.
14. Herbert Hartman, 'Prince Hal's Shewe of Zeale', *PMLA*, 46, (1931) 720.
15. Girard, p. 37.
16. J. Dover Wilson, *The Fortunes of Falstaff* (Cambridge University Press, 1964) p. 67.
17. Ibid., p. 89.
18. J. I. M. Stewart, *Character and Motive in Shakespeare* (London: Longmans, 1965) p. 138.

3 : *MEASURE FOR MEASURE* AND THE DRAMA OF PORNOGRAPHY

1. Ralph Berry, *Shakespearean Structures* (New Jersey: Barnes & Noble, 1981) p. 51.
2. L. C. Knights, 'The Ambiguity of *Measure for Measure*', *Scrutiny* 10 (1941–42) 225.
3. Meredith Skura argues that 'The real problem has to do with the larger human and social context in which such things as laws exist, and it is when the characters ignore this context, rather than when they merely indulge their appetites, that they most need correction' ('New Interpretations for Interpretation in *Measure for Measure*', *Boundary 2*, 8, ii (1979) 42.
4. A. P. Rossiter, by way of contrast, declares this speech to be hollow: 'she is too ready for the rhetorical sacrifice which has been asked of her' (*Angel With Horns* (Theatre Arts Books: New York, 1961) p. 161).
5. Philip Edwards, *Shakespeare and the Confines of Art* (London: Methuen,

　　　　1972) p. 117.
6. William Empson, *The Structure of Complex Words* (London: Chatto & Windus, 1952) p. 274.
7. Mary Lascelles, *Shakespeare's Measure for Measure* (London: Athlone Press, 1953) p. 68.
8. Coppélia Kahn, *Man's Estate: Masculine Identity in Shakespeare* (Berkley: University of California Press, 1981) p. 12.
9. F. R. Leavis, *The Common Pursuit* (Hogarth Press: London, 1984) p. 163.
10. Harriet Hawkins, *Likenesses of Truth in Elizabethan and Restoration Drama (Oxford: Clarendon Press, 1972) p. 68.*

4 : THE TRANSFORMING AUDIENCES OF *RICHARD II*

1. Wolfgang Iser, *The Implied Reader* (Baltimore: Johns Hopkins University Press, 1974) Introduction.
2. Kristian Smidt, *Unconformities in Shakespeare's History Plays* (London: Macmillan, 1982) p. 2.
3. James Winny, *The Player King: a Theme of Shakespeare's Histories* (New York: Barnes & Noble, 1968) p. 53.
4. See Peter Ure's introduction to *Richard II* (London: Methuen, 1962) p. lxxx.
5. Moody E. Prior, *The Drama of Power: Studies in Shakespeare's History Plays* (Evanston: Northwestern University Press, 1973) p. 149.
6. Smidt describes the controversy with admirable concision in his introduction to *Unconformities.*
7. John Wilders, *The Lost Garden: a View of Shakespeare's English and Roman History Plays* (London: Macmillan, 1978) p. 2.
8. Joseph A. Porter, *The Drama of Speech Acts: Shakespeare's Lancastrian Tetralogy* (Berkeley, 1979) p. 41.
9. John Baxter, *Shakespeare's Poetic Styles: Verse into Drama* (London: Routledge & Kegan Paul, 1980) p. 121.
10. Leonard Barkan, 'The Theatrical Consistency of *Richard II*', *Shakespeare Quarterly*, 19, no. 1 (1978) 5.
11. Robert Ornstein, *A Kingdom for a Stage: the Achievement of Shakespeare's History Plays* (Cambridge: Harvard University Press, 1972) p. 104.
12. Ann Righter, *Shakespeare and the Idea of the Play* (Harmondsworth, Middx: Penguin, 1962) p. 81.
13. Paul Gaudet, 'The "Parasitical" Counselors in *Richard II*', *Shakespeare Quarterly*, 33, no. 2 (1982) 154.
14. Prior, p. 174.
15. Barkan, p. 6.
16. E. M. W. Tillyard, *Shakespeare's History Plays* (Harmondsworth, Middx: Penguin, 1962), p. 246.
17. Ure, p. lxxxi.
18. A. P. Rossiter, *Angel With Horns* (New York: Theatre Arts Books, 1961) p. 24.
19. Porter, p. 140.

20. Derek Traversi, *Shakespeare: from Richard II to Henry V* (Stanford University Press, 1957) p. 39.
21. Walter Pater, *Appreciations: with an Essay on Style* (London: Macmillan, 1918) p. 198.
22. Baxter, p. 116.
23. Scott McMillin, 'Shakespeare's *Richard II*: "Eyes of Sorrow, Eyes of Desire" ', *Shakespeare Quarterly*, 35, no. 1 (1984) 45.
24. Richard D. Altick, 'Symphonic Imagery in *Richard II*', *PMLA*, 67 (1947), 364.
25. Baxter, p. 159.
26. M. M. Mahood, *Shakespeare's Wordplay* (London: Methuen, 1979) p. 88.
27. James L. Calderwood, *Shakespearean Metadrama*(University of Minnesota Press, 1971) p. 165.
28. Smidt, p. 97.
29. Righter, p. 111.
30. Marjorie Garber, ' "Vassal Actors": the Role of the Audience in Shakespearean Tragedy', *Renaissance Drama*, IX, 78.

5 : THE ALTERNATING NARRATIVES OF *TWELFTH NIGHT*

1. Ralph Berry, *The Shakespearean Metaphor* (London: Macmillan, 1978) p. 48.
2. Norman Rabkin, *Shakespeare and the Problem of Meaning* (University of Chicago, 1981) p. 34.
3. Ibid., p. 44.
4. *The Plays of William Shakespeare IV* (London, 1765) p. 123 (fn). Johnson declares that the speech 'is very artfully introduced to keep the Prince from seeming vile . . .'
5. Ifor Evans, *The Language of Shakespeare's Plays* (London: Methuen, 1964) p. 122.
6. Fredson Bowers, 'The Structure of *King Lear*', *Shakespeare Quarterly* 31, 1 (Spring 1980).
7. See John Bayley, *The Characters of Love* (London: Constable, 1960) pp. 42 *passim*.
8. Anne Barton, *'Twelfth Night' The Riverside Shakespeare*, ed. G. Blakemore Evans (Boston: Houghton Miflin, 1974) p. 404.
9. Introduction, *Twelfth Night*, eds J. M. Lothian and T. W. Craik (London: Methuen, 1975) p. lxiii.
10. Barton, p. 405.
11. Craik, p. lxiv.
12. Craik, p. lxiv.
13. Alvin Kernan, 'The Plays and the Playwrights', *The Revels History of Drama in English*, III (1576–1613) eds J. Leeds Barroll *et al.* (London: Methuen, 1975) p. 321.
14. Alexander Leggatt, *Shakespeare's Comedy of Love* (London: Methuen, 1974) p. 244.
15. Ibid., p. 244.
16. John Hollander, *'Twelfth Night* and The Morality of Indulgence', *Essays*

in Shakespearean Criticism, eds James L. Calderwood and Harold E. Toliver (Englewood Cliffs, N.J.: Prentice Hall, 1970) p. 297.

17. Ibid., p. 297.
18. Francis Fergusson, *The Idea of a Theatre* (New York: Doubleday Anchor, 1953) p. 138.
19. Ruth Nevo, *Comic Transformations in Shakespeare* (London: Methuen, 1980) p. 215.

6 : MODES OF STORY TELLING IN *OTHELLO*

1. See E. A. J. Honnigman, *Shakespeare: Seven Tragedies: the Dramatist's Manipulation of Response* (London: Macmillan, 1976) pp. 77–100.
2. In particular, see Helen Gardner, 'The Noble Moor', *Proceedings of the British Academy*, 41 (1955) pp. 189–205.
3. A. D. Nuttall, *A New Mimesis: Shakespeare and the Representation of Reality* (London and New York: Methuen, 1983) p. 134.
4. William Empson, *The Structure of Complex Words* (London: Chatto & Windus, 1951) p. 227.
5. Michael Long, *The Unnatural Scene: a Study in Shakespearean Tragedy* (London: Methuen, 1976) p. 43.
6. Catherine Shaw, ' "Dangerous Conceits Are in Their Natures Poisons": The Language of *Othello*', *University of Toronto Quarterly*, XLIX, 4 (Summer 1980) 316.
7. T. S. Eliot, *Selected Essays* (London: Faber & Faber, 1932) p. 130.
8. F. R. Leavis, *The Common Pursuit* (Harmondsworth, Middx: Penguin, 1962) p. 142.
9. Jane Adamson, *Othello as Tragedy: Some Problem of Judgement and Feeling* (Cambridge University Press, 1980) p. 28.
10. Derick C. Marsh, *Passion Lends Them Power: a Study of Shakespeare's Love Tragedies* (New York: Barnes & Noble, 1976) p. 98.
11. Barbara Everett, ' "Spanish" Othello: the Making of Shakespeare's Moor', *Shakespeare Survey 35* (Cambridge University Press, 1982) p. 110.
12. Reuben Brower, *Hero and Saint: Shakespeare and the Greco-Roman Tradition* (Oxford: Clarendon Press, 1971) p. 4.
13. Howard Felperin, *Shakespearean Representation: Mimesis and Modernity in Elizabethan Tragedy* (Princeton University Press, 1977) p. 79.
14. Nuttall, p. 139.
15. Giorgio Melchiori, 'The Rhetoric of Character Construction: *Othello*' *Shakespeare Survey 35* (Cambridge University Press, 1982) p. 66.
16. R. A. Foakes, 'Iago, Othello and the Critics', *De Shakespeare a T. S. Eliot: Melanges offerts a Henri Fluchere Etudes Anglais 63* (Paris: Didier, 1976) p. 65.
17. Nuttall, p. 139.
18. Brower, p. 9.
19. Lawrence Danson, *Tragic Alphabet: Shakespeare's Drama of Language* (New Haven, Conn.: Yale University Press, 1974) p. 120.
20. G. Wilson Knight, 'The Othello Music', *The Wheel of Fire* (London,

Faber & Faber, 1949).
21. Brian Vickers, 'Shakespeare's Hypocrites', *Daedalus*, 108 (1979) 71.
22. *Othello*, ed. M. R. Ridley (London: Methuen, 1959) p. 177.
23. Empson, p. 226.
24. See Ian Watt, *The Rise of the Novel* (University of California Press, 1967) pp. 9–35.
25. Leslie Fiedler has pointed to the comic characteristics of the first scene in *The Stranger in Shakespeare* (London: Croom Helm, 1972) p. 139.
26. Empson, p. 226.

7 : SHYLOCK AND THE IDEA OF THE JEW

1. Introduction, *The Merchant of Venice*, The Arden Edition (London: Methuen, 1964) p. xxxix.
2. Leo Kirschbaum, *Character and Characterization in Shakespeare* (Detroit: Wayne State University Press, 1962) p. 19.
3. Bernard Grebanier, interestingly enough, agrees that the play is not anti-Semitic, but contains instances of anti-Semitism. He remarks that Gratiano 'is the only character in the entire play who can be accused of anti-Semitism' (*The Truth about Shylock* (New York: Random House, 1962), p. 300).
4. Lucy S. Dawidowicz, *The War Against the Jews 1933–1945* (New York: Holt, Rinehart & Winston, 1975) p. 29.
5. Dawidowicz, p. 222.
6. John Palmer, *Political and Comic Characters of Shakespeare* (London: Macmillan, 1962) pp. 401–39: Harold C. Goddard, *The Meaning of Shakespeare* (University of Chicago Press, 1960) pp. 81–116.
7. Quoted by Lawrence Danson, *The Harmonies of the Merchant of Venice* (New Haven and London: Yale University Press, 1978) p. 130.
8. Albert Wertheim, 'The Treatment of Shylock and Thematic Integrity in *The Merchant of Venice*', *Shakespeare Studies*, 6 (1970) 75.
9. John P. Sisk, 'Bondage and Release in *The Merchant of Venice*', *Shakespeare Quarterly*, 20 (1969) 217.
10. Toby Lelyveld, *Shylock on the Stage* (Cleveland: Press of Western Reserve University, 1960) p. 8.
11. A fuller analysis of these two critical readings is provided in Danson, pp. 126–39.
12. Kirschbaum, p. 26.
13. Gordon Craig, 'Irving's Masterpiece – "The Bells",' *Laurel British Drama: The Nineteenth Century*, ed. Robert Corrigan (New York: Dell, 1967) p. 119.

8 : THE HISTORY OF *KING LEAR*

1. Fredson Bowers has argued that the climax of the story of *King Lear* is the tragic decision to divide the kingdom before the first scene. 'The Structure of *King Lear*', *Shakespeare Quarterly*, 31, 1 (Spring 1980) 16.

2. See for example F. D. Hoeniger, 'The Artist Exploring the Primitive: *King Lear*', *Some Facets of King Lear: Essays in Prismatic Criticism*, eds Rosalie Colie and F. T. Flahiff (University of Toronto Press: 1974) pp. 89–103.

3. Rosalie L. Colie, 'The Energies of Endurance: Biblical Echoes in *King Lear*', *Some Facets of King Lear*, pp. 117–45.

4. E. A. J. Honnigman, *Shakespeare: Seven Tragedies: the Dramatist's Manipulation of Response* (London: Macmillan, 1976) p. 102.

5. Robert Ornstein, 'The Ethic of the Imagination: Love and Art in *Antony and Cleopatra: Later Shakespeare: Stratford-Upon-Avon Studies 8* (New York: St. Martin's Press, 1967) p. 35.

6. John Reibetanz, *The Lear World: a Study of King Lear in its Dramatic Context* (London: Heinemann, 1977) p. 15.

7. G. Wilson Knight, *The Wheel of Fire* (London: Methuen, 1965) p. 141.

8. Lawrence Danson, *The Tragic Alphabet* (New Haven, Conn.: Yale University Press, 1974) p. 166.

9. Alvin B. Kernon, '*King Lear* and the Shakespearean Pageant of History', *On King Lear*, ed. Lawrence Danson (Princeton University Press, 1981) p. 14.

10. See James L. Jackson, ' "These same crosses . . ." ', *Shakespeare Quarterly*, 31, 3 (Autumn 1980) p. 387.

11. Sheldon Zitner, '*King Lear* and Its Language', *Some Facets of King Lear*, p. 4.

Index

Adamson, J., 89, 138n
Altick, R., 137n

Barkan, L., 55, 59, 136n
Barton, A., 77, 137n
Baxter, J., 64, 68, 136n, 137n
Bayley, J., 137n
Berry, R., 37, 72, 135n, 137n
Bowers, F., 73, 134n, 137n, 139n
Bradley, A. C., 88
Brower, R., 92, 94, 138n
Brown, J. R., 104, 105, 107

Calderwood, J., 26, 70, 135n, 137n
Carr, V., 25, 134n
Craig, Gordon, 113, 139n
Craik, T. W., 75, 77, 78, 137n
Colie, R., 140n
Council, N., 28, 135n

Danson, L., 24, 94, 121, 134n,
    138n, 140n
Dawidowicz, L., 109, 139n

Edwards, P., 43, 135n
Eliot, T. S., 89, 138n
Empson, W., 44, 88, 99, 102, 135n,
    138n
Evans, I., 73, 137n
Everett, B., 90, 138n

Felperin, H., 92, 138n
Ferguson, F., 83, 138n
Fiedler, L., 139n
Foakes, R. A., 93, 138n
Frazer, James, 134n
Frye, N., 22, 134n

Garber, M., 71, 137n
Gardner, H., 138n
Gaudet, P., 56, 136n
Girard, R., 25, 33, 135
Goddard, H., 111, 139n
Grebanier, B., 139n

Hartman, H., 31, 135n
Hawkins, H., 52, 136n
Hawkins, S., 135n
Heine, Heinrich, 111
Hibbard, G., 30, 135n
Hoeniger, F. D., 140n
Honnigman, E. A. J., 138n, 140n
Hollander, J., 83, 137n

Iser, W., 53, 136n

Jackson, J. L., 140n
Jenkins, H., 28, 134, 135n
Johnson, Samuel, 73, 137n

Kahn, C., 49, 136n
Kernan, A., 81, 131, 137n, 140n
Kirschbaum, L., 105, 112, 139n
Kittredge, G. L., 111
Knight, G. Wilson, 119, 138n, 140n
Knights, L. C., 37, 135n

Lascelles, M., 45, 136n
Leavis, F. R., 50, 89, 136n, 138n
Leggatt, A., 82, 83, 137n
Lelyveld, T., 111, 139n
Long, M., 88, 138n

Mack, M., 27, 135n
Mahood, M. M., 69, 137n
Marsh, D., 90, 91, 138n

McMillin, S., 64, 137n
Melchiori, G., 93, 138n

Nevo, R., 85, 138n
Nuttall, A. D., 88, 92, 93, 138n

Ornstein, R., 55, 119, 135n, 140n

Palmer, J., 111, 139n
Pater, Walter, 63, 137n
Porter, J., 55, 60, 136n
Prior, M. E., 54, 59, 136n

Rabkin, N., 72, 137n
Reibetanz, J., 119, 140n
Ridley, M. R., 98
Righter, A., 56, 70, 136n, 137n
Rossiter, A. P., 60, 135n

Shaw, C., 88, 138n

Sisk, J. P., 111, 139n
Skura, M., 135n
Smidt, K., 53, 70, 137n
Stewart, J. I. M., 34, 135n

Tillyard, E. M. W., 59, 136n
Traversi, D., 136n

Ure, P., 136n

Vickers, B., 95, 138n

Watt, I., 139n
Wertheim, A., 111, 139n
Wilders, J., 55, 136n
Wilson, John Dover, 33, 135n
Winny, J., 54, 136n

Zitner, S., 132, 140n